Praise for
The Transfiguration of Our World

"An inspiring and positive vision which reveals what's really going on today behind the scenes, and how we can integrate new spiritual approaches to create the future we all long for in our hearts."
— John Gray, author, *Men Are from Mars, Women Are from Venus*

"After considering the information and monumental insights in Gordon's book, *The Transfiguration of Our World*, when I wake up in the morning and hold this belief and knowing that I am part of a vast community of light helping create a transformation on our world, I feel deeply inspired. This is a completely different view of reality, and I think it is very important that everyone who is interested in the future of our planet read this book, which I will be sharing in my courses and recommending to people who are interested."
— Barbara Marx Hubbard, author, *Conscious Evolution*

"Finally, a view of world events that reveals what's going on behind the scenes! *The Transfiguration of Our World* helps us make sense of current upheavals, placing them within a vision of a world moving into a higher level of consciousness and being. Gordon shows there are spiritual beings supporting and guiding human evolution, a clear plan for how this is unfolding, and an active alliance of human and higher forces working together to transform the darkness in our world into a lighted civilization. Anyone who wants to know what's going on in the world today should read this book!"
— Marci Shimoff, #1 NY Times Bestselling author, *Happy for No Reason, Love For No Reason, Chicken Soup for the Woman's Soul*

"*The Transfiguration of Our World* is a brilliant guide to our new, lighted world. It is both beautiful and uplifting as it directly addresses how to banish forever the fear that afflicts and disempowers us in the world today. It provides a clear picture of the future we are creating from the courage

i

and love in our hearts and the spiritual help being offered to us. Read it now! Share it with everyone."

— Sonia Choquette, NY Times best-selling author,
The Answer Is Simple: Love Yourself Live Your Spirit

"This book presents an incredibly inspiring vision. I have always hoped there would be a time when Divine intervention would change the course of history - perhaps it has many times, but this takes it to another level - one that I truly hope to see happen in my lifetime. The vision of this planet fully flowering brings tears, and I can honestly say there is nothing I want more. This is a powerful book which will have a tremendous impact on human consciousness."

— Mark Krigbaum, film director, *Death Makes Life Possible*

"The truth is within this book for all to behold. The forces of light overcoming darkness is universal. What makes this book so rare and valuable is the functional and practical details of the epic story of all time Gordon has revealed from decades of work on many planes of existence. Also he connects the separate pieces of the epic story into the big picture like few others to make sense and light of our place in the universe.

The plot of this story is beyond ET, Close Encounters or Star Wars and it is real. A profound work and an action packed thriller all in one. Bring on the sequel!"

— Russell Kramer, writer

"Like many of my friends, I have really wondered what is happening in our world with all the chaos and upheaval, and where we are going in the future. I have read many books trying to answer this question, but The Transfiguration of Our World has answered this question with one of the deepest and most inspiring perspectives I have ever read.

Although this book goes far outside the box of the usual ways we think, everything shared in it intuitively rings true to me. The story of the origins of darkness on our planet, the surprising results of 9/11, the existence of a great Light Alliance helping us, and how the dark forces are being removed from our planet and the amazing future we are heading into is incredibly enlightening.

What is most powerful and inspiring of all is the understanding that we as humanity are not an isolated planet lost in space, but that we are part of a living cosmos with many other advanced civilizations supporting our growth and evolution into greater light and love. If you want to be inspired and find answers to many questions you never thought could be answered, this is the book for you."

— Nancy Barr, teacher

"This extraordinary book serves to inform humanity about the Shift on the planet we are currently engaged in from someone who has been on the cutting edge of this energy and work with humanity. Clearly written, it provides access for anyone wondering what is happening and where we are going. A must read for people who consider themselves lightworkers for the next energies streaming in."

— Suzanne Strisower, Award-winning author,
111 Inspirational Life Purpose Quotes

"'It will be a renaissance of the liberated human spirit, the likes of which has never been seen on earth.' This is one of the quotes from *The Transfiguration of Our World* that touched me at my intuitive core. A strong voice of hope and liberation is delivered in this book. It should be the #1 recommended book of the century as this is a group project for humanity and beyond."

—Catherine Finigan, spiritual leader

The Transfiguration of Our World

How a Light Alliance Is Transforming
Darkness and Creating a New Earth

GORDON ASHER DAVIDSON

Sign up for author's email list at www.worldtransfiguration.com

 Golden Firebird Press
369 3rd Street, #563
San Rafael, CA 94901

ISBN: 978-0-9835691-3-8

Cover design by Ginger Young

Dedication

To MM, MR and MDK, and all members of the Light Alliance on every dimension, whose unending love, light and spiritual power are assisting our human family to free ourselves from all dark limitations and co-create our New Earth.

Contents

Acknowledgements

This book, as with all of my work, is truly a co-creation. First and foremost, I would like to say that without my dear wife, Corinne McLaughlin, this book would not be what it is today. Her thoughtfulness and invaluable ideas, her honed editing skills and her steady, loving support have been essential to its success.

I also would not have been able to complete this book without the tireless, loving support of our ceaselessly amazing Administrative Director, Ginger Young, who contributed valuable ideas and insights for the book, designed the cover, built websites, organized seminars and balanced our finances, usually all at the same time!

And a special acknowledgment and loving appreciation is offered for all the spiritual help I have received in meditating on and writing this book. It is those beings in the spiritual dimensions who daily give me the inspiration, strength and courage to bring this work forward and provide a ceaseless waterfall of inspiration that continues to this day.

Preface to 2nd Edition

The first edition of *The Transfiguration of Our World* was published in September, 2014. Since then, there has been much progress in anchoring greater light into the world. We see more and more clearly every day the outlines of the new civilization emerging. This 2nd edition provides more examples of this, as well as updates from the Ashram of Synthesis about shifts in the plan for creating the new civilization.

This edition also includes four new chapters on Scientific Proof We Are Made of Light, Energy Flows and Galactic Alignments, Managing Overstimulation and Updates on the Plan from the inner perspective of the Ashram of Synthesis. I hope you find this useful in adding a deeper understanding to what is unfolding on our earth today.

Gordon Asher Davidson
San Rafael, California
March 1, 2015

Introduction

The Burning Ground

I never imagined when, 20 years ago, I returned to our home in our spiritual community after a meeting and found it burning up in flames that it would begin the most profound and deepest spiritual journey of my life. As my wife, Corinne, and I watched our beautiful solar home, (which had taken me three years to build), burning to the ground, along with everything we owned (except our cars), it was like being in an unreal nightmare.

In the following days we gradually went from shock to despair and then anger. Why would God allow this to happen to us? We are good spiritual people who had dedicated our lives to helping people and serving the world in any way we could. How could this be allowed to happen? I became very angry at God for laying waste to our life as we had created it.

Our home at Sirius Community and all of our files were destroyed just a week before we were to leave on a 40 city book tour launching our new book, Spiritual Politics. We had no clothes or records and we didn't even know where we were to stay on our tour. In the subsequent months, we overcame the challenges of this situation and completed our tour successfully. We were deeply moved by the help and support we received from people all over the country as we shared our story, and we also learned from other peoples' stories of recovery from loss and devastation.

We then returned to the Washington, D.C. area, where I went through a very deep process of dealing with my anger and lack of understanding of why this had happened. Before the fire, I had insisted on moving all of our belongings back to our community, after having lived and worked in Washington, D.C for some years. I found living in Washington very challenging and the energies were difficult to work with. I wanted to move back to Sirius and live in our lovely home in our peaceful, rural community.

Corinne, on the other hand, wanted to stay in Washington and felt spiritually guided to do further spiritual work there. I finally realized that my personal will to do what I wanted, rather than listening to her guidance and considering the greater good, caused this disaster to occur. At that moment, I began a struggle to release my personal will and truly surrender it to a higher spiritual Power. As I was a very willful individual, this was a process that continued for some months. Finally, I was able to let go, and to say (and really mean), "Not my will but Thine." Our fire had taught me the power of spiritual fire.

At that point I had my first direct, clairvoyant contact with a spiritual Master on the inner planes. This began a deep, 20 year process of being guided and inspired by members of the Master's ashram on the inner dimensions of life. All the initiatives, books and projects I have undertaken since that time have been the result of this inner guidance and direction, which has proved to be invaluable in my life and work.

The Source of This Book

The Transfiguration of Our World is based on the results of these 20 years of contact and inner telepathic guidance from a Master in the inner Ashram of Synthesis, which I regularly share with an international group actively serving in many capacities around the world. This Master is deeply involved at a high level of leadership in the unfoldment of the plan for our world.

The Ashram of Synthesis is a group of Masters and spiritual beings on the inner levels of consciousness who are focused on the higher evolutionary plan for helping humanity liberate itself and fulfill its full potential. Masters are souls who have reincarnated through many lives on earth, learned and mastered all the lessons of earth life, and no longer need to reincarnate. They are dedicated to inspiring humanity through a positive vision of our future, and showing us how we can mature spiritually to create the future we all long for in our hearts.

I have done my very best to allow the communication to be as clear and accurate as possible. Through learning from past doubts and errors, after many years I have truly honed my receptive telepathic skills. I always carefully run everything by my heart intuition and also see if what I receive is real, practical and makes sense to me. I am confident that a very high percentage of what I am sharing here is accurate as to the vision and plan of the Ashram and higher levels of consciousness.

The content of this book is the distilled result of hundreds of these two way conversations with the Master, especially over the past two years. I also use his feedback to verify the truth of research I do on the internet on these topics. There are a number of people around the world who are receiving similar information, much of which correlates with what I am receiving.

The information presented here was shared with an international group in an invitational monthly teleseminar which began on September 30, 2013, and continued for nine months. A second teleseminar began in the Fall of 2014, which is open to all those who are familiar with this book, and video recordings are available. These teleseminars present the unfolding higher plan for the transfiguration of our world and how we can raise our frequency to cooperate with this plan. Transfiguration is the full reception and integration of the vast waves of inflowing light and love pouring into our planet. This light is creating a new humanity and a new earth, which is emerging as we live in higher dimensional consciousness while still being present in our bodies in the physical world.

All that is being offered here should be taken into the light of your own soul and intuition and evaluated, keeping what resonates as useful to you, and letting go of the rest. I encourage an active and open dialogue with those who study this material. Each session includes a meditation on the themes and ideas presented. This book also explores the deeper side of world events and how the plan is being unfolded in the modern world.

Much of the material here is new, and may even be challenging to existing beliefs you hold. All I ask is that you give everything careful consideration and allow insight and new perspectives to arise from the cumulative ideas of each chapter, which you are always free to accept or not.

The purpose of this book is to transmit to you my understanding of the current energies, ideas and goals of the higher plan held by the Ashram of Synthesis. The goal is to facilitate, to whatever degree you choose, an integration of these energies of love, light and will more fully into all levels of your being, to help you be more radiant and potent in your life and service.

The Potential Impact of This Book

This book is a modern expression of what is known as the Ageless Wisdom or Perennial Philosophy, which has appeared throughout the ages, cloaked in the fabric of each civilization and culture, from ancient India, Egypt, Persia, and Greece into the modern era. This version is being given at this time of transformation in human history to meet humanity's need to know the deeper causes of the current conditions on earth, what is being done co-creatively by humanity and the spiritual Powers to transform our world, and the goals and plan for the unfolding new civilization. It is a corrective lens for humanity's vision of the future, which, despite dark scenarios being imagined by some, is a future filled with light, joy and great creative unfoldment for humanity and all life on our planet.

The course correction currently being applied by humanity and the spiritual Powers working heart-to-heart and hand-in-hand together will guide our civilization into a new life for our world, where our planet and all life upon it will be living in alignment with cosmic principles, and actively co-creating with galactic life itself.

The current response to the multidimensional crisis which all life on earth is passing through is a purifying of the dark history of earth and a cleansing of negative energies anchored within the very substance of the earth. It is removing all dark, controlling forces who have failed in their attempt to dominate and rule the earth for their own selfish purposes. The story of their origins, the creation of their control systems, and their ultimate undoing and removal from power is clearly outlined in this book.

It is the story of the triumph of the human spirit and the truly indomitable power of freedom when allied with spiritual forces in the cosmos who seek the liberation of all beings into their fullest Divine potential. It is the story of what is unfolding right now, today, on planet earth.

All that is occurring today is a result of the interaction of human free will choices with the higher plan. Today that plan and the goals outlined here are being co-created through world events. Each of us, and all of humanity who love their fellow beings and life on earth, has a part to play and a contribution to make to this unfolding plan. This book will give you understanding, vision and inspiration. It will provide the tools of consciousness to discover your Divine purpose and play your part in the great symphony of the whole.

What you hold in your hands is not simply a book. It is an energetic package, which when opened and read, will have an explosive impact on your consciousness. You have decided to explore this book because you have a resonance with the theme and are drawn to the ideas it presents. This means you are ready to enter into the state of awareness which this book will bring to you.

The Changing Energies on Earth

Many of us around the world intuit in our hearts, minds, and souls that the world is going through a tremendous transformation, as there are positive solutions to previously frozen world problems emerging everywhere. People are waking up and taking bold and creative action to address the issues of our times.

Many are sensing that the energies within and around us are rising to a higher frequency every day. They are beginning to feel lighter and more energized. Many are also noticing they are finding it easier to contact the subtle spiritual worlds, as they seem closer to us, and the barriers to reaching them seem reduced. Worldwide meditations are proliferating all over the world to support and distribute the higher energies pouring into our planet. Greater light and love is permeating everywhere, yet many people may not fully understand what is causing this transformation and where it is leading us.

Understanding the Livingness of the Plan

There is no topic more important to all of us than having a deeper understanding of the current unfoldment of the Divine plan. Earth itself is a living being, as is the great Being whose body is our solar system. The plan is the higher purpose, vision and goals for the earth and humanity held by these great spiritual beings, who are incarnated as our earth and our solar system, holding in their consciousness the next steps for all life on earth.

The unfolding of the plan is a coordinated focusing of light, love and power from the forces of light in multiple dimensions. This includes humanity (embodying creative intelligence), the spiritual hierarchy of Masters (as a heart center of love/wisdom), and Shamballa, (the center where the will of God is known). In addition there is active engagement of the angelic and devic kingdoms, the Mother of the World (the being whose body is the substance of earth or Gaia) and the Father of the World, (the being who initiated the creation of the earth and holds it in manifestation), and galactic civilizations organized as the Galactic Light Alliance. Each sphere of life has its own central focalizing presence, and are all held within the infinitely vast field of the Source/ Creator whom we call God, the One Life or the Universe.

We need to know what the current short and long term goals of the plan are, how these are being implemented and what we each can do to help it unfold. The Divine plan is a living plan and is constantly being changed and adapted based on the inflow of new energies and always dynamic world conditions, which are very different now than they were in the past.

In my understanding from the guidance I have received, the plan for the transfiguration of our world is the plan for the infusion of light and love into the actual substance of the earth and all beings living upon it, including the nature kingdoms. This will raise the entire world to a more spiritual state of being.

This parallels the process that Jesus went through, called the transfiguration, the powerful experience when he was radiant with light on the mountaintop. It is the future of our planet to similarly be radiant with this great spiritual light and love.

This requires the fullest possible participation of every individual and group, by opening to the higher light of transfiguration, and allowing this light to enter all dimensions of our beings. As this light is absorbed, it reconfigures our energy system, and raises the vibrational frequency of our atomic substance, including our DNA.

This allows us each to become ever greater radiating beacons of light in a rapidly transfiguring world. We will be discussing and working with all these ideas in depth throughout this book. I invite you to evaluate all you read here through your own intuition, and let your own inner wisdom be your guide, as I do not claim any ultimate authority for what I am sharing here. It is my deepest intention that this book will be a helpful guide and inspiration for co-creating a transfigured, joyful world for you and all life on earth.

Gordon Asher Davidson
San Rafael, California
August 10, 2014

Section I

Love, Light and Darkness
in our Solar System

Chapter 1

Opening Portals into
The Matrix of Love

Love, even as it is most deeply understood, is much more than is usually considered. The spiritual hierarchy (the evolved Masters and higher beings who guide and overlight humanity and the earth) does not experience love as just an energy that can be called upon to sweeten or clarify relationships, or that stimulates, warms and opens hearts, or brings the energy of repentance, forgiveness and lasting connection — although it provides all of these.

Love is an all pervading, omnipresent, infinite field matrix of energy which transcends all dimensional limitations of time and space and creates an indissoluble bond between all worlds and dimensions. It is an energetic matrix which, when entered at any point in any dimension, ultimately unfolds into a unity of consciousness with ever expanding wholes, to which there is no end or limit.

Love is the greatest expander and extender of consciousness there is, the link between all the worlds and dimensions. It is the ever present matrix which holds every atom and every galaxy in right relationship. As such, entering the matrix through any dimensional portal intimately and ultimately leads into an ever expanding revelation of the seamless unity of the whole, which is the One Life.

Thus, the task of unfoldment for each individual unit of life is to discover their unique portal of entry into this matrix of love, the One Life. The point of entry can be love for oneself, one's family, group, nation or the world.

Once entered, the matrix steadily and naturally expands the focus of love, its reach and inclusive embrace, ultimately to all the worlds. In this understanding is hidden the secret of the human heart, and its capacity to endlessly expand into the Whole.

This is why the mind without the unfoldment of the heart is incomplete and ultimately limited by the power of its own thought forms. (These thoughtforms are crystallized patterns of thought that circulate through our minds, and become an energetic barrier that can block the entrance of higher truths and experiences.)

The mind and its thoughtforms cannot transcend themselves without the realizations discovered by entering the matrix of love. This explains why the opening to love is an ultimate opening to all of humanity and to the entire planet, and finally to the Universe and its unlimited Presence.

The source of love is innate within the nature of Divinity itself. When any contact or opening to love is made, a portal of resonance with this Divine Presence and Reality is opened, which elevates and transforms the nature of the one who opens. One then enters into the potential to ultimately know and experience the great matrix of love that extends infinitely in all dimensions and worlds.

Each of our entire multi-dimensional beings is like a giant tuning fork which has the potential to resonate with any frequency. When we resonate with love at any entry point, we enter this field matrix of love. The chakras are centers for this energy reception and expression, and their degree of development and openness influences our capacity to receive and radiate love.

However, an individual's entire etheric, emotional or mental body can also resonate to the love frequency, and thus an entry into the love matrix is created. This occurs even if the chakras are not opened or developed, although the full reception and expression of love requires this development. This is how less developed people can be influenced by love and helped to understand it.

(See end of Section I for a reflective exercise on the Matrix of Love).

Chapter 2

The Hidden History of Our Earth

Introductory Comments

Gaining a true understanding of the inner, hidden history of earth and humanity is a potent and deep initiation into the mysteries of life. In exploring this topic, it is important to remember that the forces of light are always more powerful than the forces of darkness, and in fact are the primary power in our system. They are the originators of the plan for the transfiguration of our world.

In the Ageless Wisdom tradition, it is said that the spiritual hierarchy (the Masters and enlightened beings) came to earth millions of years ago, and have guided and assisted humanity at every step of our evolution. And one of their major tasks throughout humanity's evolution has been to offset the activities and influence of what is known as the dark lodge. From many teachings, we know much about the spiritual hierarchy and the Masters and higher Beings who work with them, but very little about the origins and workings of the dark lodge.

This was intentional by the Masters, and we are now entering deeply into this topic because humanity is ready to understand the activities and impact of these dark forces in our world. While we are each responsible for transforming our own shadow aspects, our individual darkness, it is important that good spiritual people understand the larger forces of darkness in our world today beyond our personal unresolved issues. These larger dark forces feed off the collective dark impulses within humanity, which is why it is so important for us to work on our own transformation.

We live in the third dimension of a planet of duality, created by God or Spirit for our spiritual growth — so we can experience the opposites, learning to appreciate them all, and then transcending these temporary three dimensional dualities in our culture, politics, religions, etc. We have to learn to recognize darkness or harmful thoughts and actions, and to freely choose good instead.

There is a state of non-duality, beyond good and evil, (often called the 4th or 5th dimensions) embodied by enlightened Masters throughout history. They have fully overcome the challenges of the darkness within themselves, and they tirelessly work to offset the larger evil in our world. But we must remember it is not possible for us to transcend what we have not fully understood.

The dark lodge is a group of beings who are completely dedicated to controlling and dominating the world for their own exploitative and dark purposes, with absolutely no respect for human free will or human life. The agents and outer organization of this inner dark lodge are often popularly called "the cabal."

Exploring what the dark lodge really is can confront us with very potent truths that might inspire fear, a sense of overwhelm or other emotions. This is one of the reasons that we have begun this book with a strong focus on the matrix of love, its function and how to access it. This will help us to maintain this loving field as we explore this intense but very significant and necessary topic.

The information you will find in this book will help you understand earth's history, the causes of current conditions in the world, and the forces behind events in a completely new light. This perspective will likely challenge many of the assumptions you have held about "how the world is." I invite you to approach this topic with an open heart and mind and with the fearlessness and courage of a spiritual warrior, knowing you always have the backing of the spiritual Masters and the forces of light in a loving and benevolent Universe.

The Galactic Wars and Formation of the Light Alliance

The history of our galaxy, for very long cycles of time, has been fraught with interplanetary conflicts and wars. Great and terrible destructive weapons were used to attack and destroy whole civilizations. After centuries of great battles between positive civilizations that honored free will and the evolution of all races and civilizations, and those darker civilizations that sought to conquer, exploit and enslave others, the light forces gained supremacy throughout the galaxy. The various existing alliances were ultimately woven into what is called the Galactic Light Alliance, also known as the Galactics.

The Light Alliance is based on an agreement to keep the peace and uphold the principles of freedom, self-chosen development and evolution, and friendly relations between all races and civilizations. The degree of contact is entirely left to each race and planet, although peaceful nonviolent criteria are required. Those planets still struggling to achieve this degree of consciousness are carefully protected and often supported to evolve to this stage of maturity.

Many of these galactic civilizations live and function on multiple dimensions, and some focus very little, if at all, on the three physical dimensions. This is why planets appear to be uninhabited, which is not true in reality. Mercury, Saturn, and Jupiter, for example, have active and highly evolved civilizations present.

Other planets such as Uranus and Pluto have the function of relating to the larger galaxy and transmitting these energies to planets in our solar system. All of this ordered Divine activity takes place within the body of the Solar Logos (the being whose body of manifestation is the planets of our system) and the Grand Heavenly Being, (the being made up of seven solar systems), of which ours is one. This beautiful, Divine order is governed by the spiritual principle that the microcosm always reflects the macrocosm and vice versa.

The reason that information about galactic civilizations has been suppressed by governments and the media is not just because this information is outside the normal paradigm and might frighten people. More importantly, it is it is because the dark forces, who have mostly controlled the media and many governments, know the Galactics recognize and oppose them, and are the only power capable of overthrowing their dark rule of this planet.

The Disruption of the Plan for Earth/Gaia

Earth, often referred to as "Gaia," was conceived of and created as an ultimate expression of physical beauty, abundance and joy that was meant to be shared by all lives present upon it. It was protected by the Light Alliance guardians and other spiritual beings overlighting its evolution.

However, no protection is absolute, and due to an unprecedented anomaly in the time/space continuum millennia ago, a certain group of a predatory alien race was able to enter from another dimension and establish itself on earth with the intention of colonizing its resources and people for their own uses. For a very brief period they were able to conceal themselves from the guardians of the Light Alliance.

The Function of the Dark Forces in the Plan

Once their infiltration was discovered, the question arises why they were not removed, as this was the beginning of many millennia of a long, painful period in earth's history.

The answer is that this invasion was ultimately recognized and accepted in Shamballa (the council of enlightened beings which holds the purpose and plan for all life on earth) as part of the higher plan. This decision was made after much careful debate in the Shamballa council, with the assumption that struggling against these dark forces would strengthen and empower humanity.

The alien invaders were allowed to remain because it was decided that providing each human soul the opportunity to make a choice between the higher path of light and the lower path of darkness would stimulate the most evolutionary growth. As karma (or the results of the choices made by each soul) unfolded from the sum of the thoughts, words and actions chosen and expressed by each soul, many lessons and understandings of universal spiritual truths would emerge.

Was this a correct assumption? Ultimately, yes, but it took longer and required special assistance to become a positive factor in human evolution. The nature of this special assistance will be explained as we proceed.

The Formation of the Dark Lodge

The original alien group of about 50 beings steadily expanded their influence over humans by demonstrating their superior powers, and they gradually established the dark lodge on earth. They were not able to reproduce among themselves, but they ultimately interbred with humans, as they had the ability to shape shift and appear to be human. This eventually resulted in powerful ruling groups or planetary elites, (popularly known as the cabal), who are cooperating with the dark aliens, and have various levels of awareness of who they are actually working with.

Some of the other powers of the dark ones allowed them to exert very powerful telepathic control and dominance over ordinary human beings. They also could see into the future for a certain cycle, although not to an unlimited degree.

Mechanisms of the Cabal's Control

Using human agents, either under their control, or voluntarily cooperating with their displays of power, the intruding aliens steadily established their centers of influence and control on inner and outer planes.

Beginning in Lemuria, (a very ancient civilization lost to history) and developed further in Atlantis, (the continent that existed in the mid-Atlantic in ancient times), they employed psychotronic technologies, using combined psychic and technological means on the inner planes to create veils around the planet.

By the use of these psychotronic veils, they were able to reduce the capacity of human DNA to absorb and radiate light, by shielding human DNA from the inflow of light which is always present. For most individ-

7

uals, these veils also blocked or limited access to the higher spiritual planes of consciousness, except for those who were strongly motivated to break through them.

These are the veils that many spiritual teachings refer to, but are never clearly explained as to what they are or how they came to exist, as humanity has not been ready for this knowledge. They function by keeping humanity within the "halls of maya" — immersed in the physical dimension as the only reality — or imprisoned on the astral/emotional plane of desire through fear and controlling thoughtforms.

Interbreeding with humans allowed the invaders, their offspring and cooperators to ultimately establish, over very long periods of time, a vast network of control systems that function in the modern world through financial and political power, the media, interlocking corporate directorates, as well as through assassination, bribery and intimidation of political leaders.

Chapter 3

The Struggle Between the Light and Dark Forces

The aliens first came to earth during the Lemurian period, which was many millennia ago. The spiritual Masters began opposing them from the very beginning of their intrusion. However, they could not be completely stopped or removed because the spiritual Masters guiding the earth did not have the power nor permission to remove them, as it had been determined that these dark forces would be part of earth's evolutionary process.

The Masters opposed them by implanting the teachings of light, love and higher purpose in every civilization and culture throughout the ages, inspiring all who were open to them. And thus, ever since, there has been a great battle for the minds, hearts and souls of humanity.

This has allowed humanity to evolve by choosing between the ways of light or darkness, and learning from the karma of their choices. The growth and unfoldment of humanity has proceeded, although slowly, with a more deeply embedded understanding of why it is necessary and beneficial to all (including oneself) to choose the lighted, loving path. This has also greatly developed the potential of humanity to assist other civilizations to move through a similar process in the future.

The presence of the dark ones in Lemuria resulted in conflicts between Lemuria and Atlantis, and eventually the Lemurian civilization disappeared. The dark ones then gradually infiltrated Atlantis, corrupting it and eventually taking it over. They knew much about genetic manipulation and created many hideous life forms. They tried to interfere with humanity's DNA, but were not completely successful, due to the protection of humanity by their Solar Angels, the angelic presence that is with each person, known as our "Guardian Angel."

All the civilizations begun after Atlantis — Tibet, Central America, Egypt — began as a pure impulse, creating a high point of civilization, but gradually they were infiltrated by human agents of the dark ones. These reincarnated human dark ones were from Atlantis and other times, and their karmic line of least resistance again brought them into resonance with the dark overlords, the invading aliens. They were given direct instructions and goals to achieve in corrupting and manipulating these civilizations, especially the priests and political leaders.

Ultimately, Atlantis became so corrupted it was destroyed. When Atlantis was inundated by the flood, (as described in the Bible and other spiritual teachings), the human cooperators with the dark lodge were destroyed, but not the originating dark group, as they were embedded on the inner planes.

World War II

Many centuries later, World War II was another attempt by these same alien dark ones, who controlled Hitler and the Nazis, to take over the planet as a whole. In the monumental struggle with the spiritual forces of light, the dark ones nearly won, but help from beyond the earth was given to the Allied powers. This help, according to the information I received from the Ashram in meditation, came from Galactic civilizations — from Sirius, the Pleiades and Arcturus.

Although the Galactic civilizations did not directly intervene, they provided the energy for the Allies, the spiritual Masters and Shamballa to hold the point of spiritual tension and thus outlast and defeat the dark forces. The Galactics were not permitted to intervene directly at that time, as the goal was to maintain a balance between the spiritual Hierarchy and the dark lodge, so that humanity would have to choose between them and act, which they did.

There also was a race with the dark ones for the development of the atomic bomb, and the Galactics prevented the Axis powers from accessing the secrets of atomic energy and using it more extensively than the Allies.

With the defeat of the Axis powers, many of their human cooperators were destroyed, but the dark lodge was not fully eliminated. They were temporarily driven behind the "door where evil dwells," (a specific location on the inner planes where they were sealed) and remained. It was then humanity's responsibility to keep this door closed by not being open to harmful values, attitudes and actions, but it has not been able to do so.

The United Nations was the spiritual hierarchy's attempt, after the war, to establish a world government of light. It has been partially successful, despite some infiltration by the dark ones.

The Modern Plan for Domination of the Earth

As the influence and control of the dark lodge reemerged after World War II and grew in the modern world, plans were put in place for ever greater domination and exploitation of humanity. One of these was to reduce the population of the earth by 80% for easier control. This was to be carried out though nuclear war, epidemics like the SARS virus, and other means.

The staged destruction of the Twin Trade towers and other buildings in New York on 9/11 was intended to create an event which would instill great fear and justify removing many freedoms and protections of U.S. citizens. It would allow the installation of ever greater controls in the name of "homeland security." This plan was successful in creating greater fear and control, but it had massive unforeseen consequences for the dark lodge.

Chapter 4

The Consequences of 9/11 and the Spiritual Decrees

In 2002, one year after the 9/11 attack, the council of the Solar Logos, and the Universal council of the Heavenly Being, (which includes the seven solar systems of which ours is one), realized that the complete control of earth by the dark lodge was imminent, and humanity, Hierarchy and Shamballa together could not stop it.

Because the earth is a chakra within the body of the Solar Logos, as are all the planets, this dark condition of earth was, under the Law of Progression, holding back the forward evolution of our solar system. As a result, it was affecting the evolution of the Heavenly Being, and even this entire area of the galaxy.

The Law of Progression states that when an entity moves forward into a higher frequency of energy and expanded state of consciousness, all bodies and lesser entities within it must also move upward. But because of the dark control of earth, the earth was not able to move upward and was thus retarding the progression of the entire solar system, with a ripple effect into this quadrant of the galaxy.

As a result, a great decision was made, and a decree from the Universal and Solar councils was issued which stated that humanity and earth would be freed from all control or influence of the dark forces, and the alien entities would be completely removed from the planet. Assistance from higher Light Forces would be given to achieve this goal in a relatively short period of time.

The decree also stated that an increased and intensified radiation of light and active assistance would be given to the earth and humanity by spiritual forces, including other galactic civilizations. The galactic civilizations were given permission to actively intervene, using their spacecraft and advanced technologies, to prevent the worst plans of the cabal from being fulfilled. One of the dark plans included creating a worldwide nuclear war started in the Middle East, which was intended to radically reduce the population.

The dark ones and their cooperators planned to live in vast, underground cities around the world until the radiation subsided, and then rule the world with the remaining population as their slaves. This plan was terminated by the galactic civilizations through closing down these bases and preventing any nuclear exchanges. Another part of the solar decree also states that no major nuclear explosions or nuclear war will be allowed on earth.

The Galactics, who have inconceivably more advanced technologies than ours, also neutralized the SARS virus, which was another dark plan to reduce the population. The Galactics are also supporting the light factions in every institution, including the U.S. military. The percentage of those in the leadership of the military supporting some aspect of the higher plan (based on their level of understanding), has now grown to about 85%.

These decrees and direct actions were known as a possibility by the spiritual Masters, but the timing was not. The Masters have been working closely with all these efforts, and they are completely coordinated through Shamballa, with specific groups acting from within the Ashram of Synthesis.

An Exponential Awakening

As more of humanity awakens, demanding and creating change, the Galactics and other higher light forces have increasing freedom to help us, as our free will choices and intentions to be free of all dark control are aligning with the plan. This allows them to increasingly intervene to prevent any major initiatives for disruption and destruction.

The Galactics have greatly reduced and neutralized the chemicals within the chemtrail spraying, the trails from airplanes that sometimes cloud our skies. They are also neutralizing nuclear radiation from Fukushima in Japan and other locations, and they are cleaning the seas and the air. They are supporting all positive individuals and groups within the system working at any level for progress towards the higher plan.

The severe and unusual weather causing drought, floods and storms is part of the purification process of the earth, and is not directly a result of cabal activities.

The decree of the Universal and Solar councils also permitted the removal of the leaders of the dark lodge. The 50 original aliens who founded the dark lodge are no longer on earth. Each one was given the opportunity to turn to the light, after being held accountable for their crimes. If they did not choose to turn and be reeducated, they were removed from any further contact with earth.

Much of the confusion we see in the world today is because the remaining leaders of the cabal have lost their controlling dark guides, who had greater powers and an overview of all conditions on earth. The remaining leaders have no one to tell them what to do, so they are confused and spiraling down into infighting, self-protection and fear for their lives. But many are also turning towards the light.

(We will discuss further stages of the unfolding plan of transfiguration in upcoming chapters, including detailed understanding of how the plan is being worked out in the modern world.)

Reflective Exercise on Portals into the Matrix of Love

- Meditate on love as an all pervading, omnipresent, infinite field matrix of energy which transcends all dimensional limitations of time and space, creating an indissoluble bond between all worlds and dimensions.
- Experience love as an energetic matrix which, when entered at any point in any dimension, ultimately unfolds into a unity of consciousness with ever expanding wholes, to which there is no end or limit.
- Experience love as the greatest expander and extender of consciousness there is, the link between all the worlds and dimensions, the ever present matrix which holds every atom and every galaxy in right relationship.
- As such, entering the matrix through any dimensional portal intimately and ultimately leads into an ever expanding revelation of the seamless unity of the whole — the One, the One Life.
- Recognize that true love can overcome the darkness within ourselves and help transform the organized darkness in the world.

The following are questions which you may like to consider about the portals you use to enter into the Matrix of Love:

1. What are your most open portals for you to access the love matrix?
2. How consciously do you use them? How often?
3. How deeply do you expand into the matrix of love when you enter it?
4. What do you learn there?
5. What do you need to do to always remain inside or within the threshold of this portal, and therefore always within the love matrix?
6. How can you share your portals of entry with others and discover what works best for them?
7. How can you heal your fear of the darkness within yourself and in the world using the power of love?

Section II

Using Light to Transform Darkness

Chapter 5

Working with the Properties of Light

As we have been discussing the Light Alliance, it is important to understand the properties of light and how light can adapt and mold itself to different uses and applications. In its essence, light can function both as a particle and/or as a wave. As a wave, light serves to radiate light energy and illuminate all the subplanes of existence from the physical to the atmic plane.

All seven planes of existence, the physical/etheric, astral/emotional, mental, buddhic/intuitional, atmic/spiritual, monadic, and divine/logoic are subdivided into 7 subplanes, making 49 subplanes in all. The atmic plane is the plane of pure, spiritual will, the buddhic is compassion and spiritual insight, the monadic is the plane of oneness, and the divine is the plane of the Source/Creator.

As a particle, light condenses into light substance, the inner light energy which substands and allows the creation of all form. It supports the stability and continuity of all forms in the worlds, until the life within the form is withdrawn.

Light as a healing agent reorganizes bodies, organs, cells, atoms and DNA, replacing what is outworn, outmoded and ready to be released, allowing a higher frequency of light to be present.

Light is also the conveyor of atomic substance, which is the substance carrying the higher frequencies of the atmic (will) and buddhic (intuitive wisdom) planes.

Light conveys this substance by functioning as a carrier wave for it, and with its adaptability it can mold itself to vibrate to these higher frequencies and bring them into contact with the three bodies (physical/etheric, emotional and mental) of human beings.

As the frequencies of our bodies rise, and our percentage of light substance increases, we become an embodied transmitter of light without any effort or specific action. We become a point of light within a greater light. This light is also a field, and it is accessed through the focused use of our mind, synthesized with love.

The Manifestations of Light in Our Bodies

Light has various manifestations. There is light within our etheric or energy body which brings vitality, health and unimpeded circulation to all organs and cells resulting in a radiant health.

There is light within our astral or emotional body, which brings sensitivity to beauty, to other people, life forms and to the far-off spiritual worlds, as well as intuitive understanding and joy, when it is fully integrated. There is the light of love within our heart, which brings unity with others and ultimately with the whole.

Light in our mental body brings revelation and understanding of principles, the capacity for abstract thought, recognition of the moral order of the universe and one's place within it. Thus we can see the effects of light on our different bodies.

Transfiguration and the New Earth

Transfiguration is the raising of the vibrational frequency of matter, including the subtle bodies of humanity, the nature kingdoms and the entire earth itself. Transformation is changing the form, while Transfiguration is a refiguring and raising of the essential, inner energies within a form. As these frequencies are raised into a higher dimensional vibration through the absorption of light and love, the spiritual worlds become perceptible as a realm of experience for humanity.

This is achieved by allowing the infusion of light, love and higher purpose into consciousness, and into the subtle and dense bodies of human beings and nature. Nature itself has already made this shift into a higher frequency, which is popularly known as the fifth dimension.

This infusion of higher energies allows all life to function within more subtle spiritual levels, while also retaining the capacity to function in the physical, emotional and mental worlds. When this is fully accomplished, we will have a transfigured world, both within humanity and within nature. This is the purpose and immediate goal of the plan. It will give greatly expanded space for the creative expression of human free will, guided and held within the matrix of love.

Each individual is using their free will choice to decide if they intend to function within the matrix of love or not. This choice determines the frequency and quality of the environment which they will inhabit. Allowing people to find their own level and make choices to move to a higher one is the essence of the higher plan.

Everything happens within Divine law and order, determined by the free will choices of humanity. The plan simply sets the vast parameters and principles of how those free will choices create their inevitable results. All this occurs through the law of karma, which requires that for each choice and action there is an equal response of the same frequency and quality of the choices made. The new earth will be the condition and quality of the human and natural environment when light, love and higher will frequencies are anchored and the planet is transfigured.

(See end of Section II for a meditation on Light).

Chapter 6

The Plan for the Elimination of the Dark Lodge

The Impact of the Universal Decree on the Dark Lodge

All the plans of the dark lodge were disrupted by the recent decree from the Universal council of the Heavenly Being (whose body consists of seven solar systems) and the Solar Logos of our solar system which decreed their removal from the earth. Due to the control of earth by the dark lodge, the blocked evolution of our planet (which is a chakra in the body of our solar system), was delaying the evolution of the solar system and all seven solar systems of the Heavenly Being, and even beyond.

The flow of energies throughout the universe is directed through a series of ever greater councils, with energies from the larger whole being consciously received and then released through this series of councils. This transmits the energies and impulses which guide the evolution of each level of the system. Thus, in our system, the Universal council of the Heavenly Being (made up of seven solar systems) transmits energy to the Solar council (guiding our solar system), which transmits it to Shamballa (the council holding the plan for our earth), which then transmits it to the inner ashrams of spiritual Masters, who transmit it to the worldwide group of light workers (the Earth Light Alliance) who assist the unfolding plan on earth.

The decree stating that earth and humanity must be freed from control of the dark forces began a gradually more direct engagement of galactic civilizations in breaking down the control systems of the dark lodge. It countered their plans and activities, such as neutralizing the SARS virus and preventing nuclear war in the Middle East.

The Light Alliance has also neutralized the dark lodge's plans to create other "false flag" events like 9/11 which result in further chaos and fear and facilitate their control. They have neutralized many forms of pollution, and are holding the earth in balance to minimize the effects of seismic and weather events, and are supporting the courageous whistleblowers and truth researchers who are exposing the activities of the dark lodge.

Balancing Human Free Will and Higher Help

As a principle, it is important that human free will demonstrates efforts to oppose the dark forces and that humanity struggles to become free.

There is a careful balancing of intervention by the Galactics and the Masters and the efforts by humanity, so that the help given does not disempower or weaken humanity. However, the forces controlling humanity were so great and so locked in place, that assistance was needed to break the stalemate between the light and dark forces on earth.

Humanity, Hierarchy and Shamballa together were struggling to prevent the complete takeover and control of the planet by the dark forces, but they were not able to drive them from the planet. This is now occurring because of the decree and the help of the galactic civilizations.

The decree came in part because the painful condition of earth was having an effect throughout the Heavenly Being and beyond, since pain and suffering anywhere vibrates throughout the matrix of love.

This painful condition was allowed to go on for so long to work out the karma of many souls involved. Shamballa and Hierarchy did all they could to prevent even worse outcomes, until the higher decrees were made. The Masters knew the decrees might happen at some unknown point in the future, because they had been promised that the battle and stalemate with the dark lodge would not go on indefinitely.

Containment

One of the methods used to control the cabal and create change is containment. Containment is a process of surrounding dark individuals or groups with a type of light box which suffuses them with love, and causes their dark thoughts and plans to instantly rebound on them. They are sealed in these boxes, and their negative thoughts and energies cannot escape or impact the world.

This is implemented primarily by the Archangels and Angels, and is done by decree. The containment is like a box or a sphere, depending on the individual. The densest individuals require a box, and lighter ones a sphere, and all negative energies bounce back on them. In the more extreme cases, they are held there continually penetrated by love and light until the purification is complete, and they alter their way of responding to the world.

Well known leaders in the world have been in containment for varying periods of time, including many members of the powerful financial elites, banking families and political leaders. Shifts in several countries are due to containment of leaders there, and are part of the Plan for creating the necessary conditions for peace in the world,

We might ask, if this is being done, why are there still so many tragic events that seem very much like dark forces operations? These are due to patterns that were put in motion in the past that are still unfolding. And many of these situations are allowing the karma of those involved to be worked out, thus freeing them in the future.

Events like mass shootings (when they are not false flag staged events) are done by programmed, robotized people manipulated by different elements of the cabal acting independently as the entire system breaks down. This is allowed because a degree of free will still must be permitted to work out karma. It is also allowed so that people will stand up and demand that such things be stopped.

The Breakdown of the Cabal

The cabal is the outer structure and organization of the inner forces known as the dark lodge. The command and control within the cabal is breaking down, with only about 35% remaining, and that is fading. This is happening because the cabal has been cut off from its alien leadership and its unlimited sources of money, and because its human members are turning to the Light, or are trying to protect themselves by disconnecting from the cabal.

The dark lodge is thus losing the mechanism for its stranglehold on humanity in the three dimensions — the physical, emotional, and the mental — through its fading control over the life of humanity. Over the next period this will be completely broken down, as its bases on the mental plane are being broken up and dispersed.

The original aliens who founded the dark lodge have been removed from the planet. There are many of their human offspring still present, but many are turning to the light, and others are being removed.

Cabal members will be held accountable for their actions, and the equivalent of a Truth and Reconciliation commission will be established to encourage forgiveness by humanity. Humanity will be taught by new, lighted leaders that even those who have committed the worst of crimes deserve love and forgiveness. Being able to hold this loving and wise consciousness, despite all the terrible crimes by the cabal, will be a great achievement and initiation for humanity.

The Ashram assures us that we will inevitably be successful at completely eliminating the dark forces' control of the planet, and we will see this clearly in the near future. At the right time, we will have disclosure of the existence of galactic civilizations and their relationship to earth and humanity, followed by Ascension or Transfiguration, which will allow our consciousness to rise into the higher dimensions. This means that our consciousness will be able to function freely on the higher planes while still being able to live in our physical bodies.

Chapter 7

Coordination of the Unfolding Plan of Transfiguration

The unfolding of the plan is a coordinated focusing of light, love and power from the forces of light in multiple dimensions. These include the center, humanity (the creative throat center), the spiritual hierarchy of Masters (the heart center of love wisdom), and Shamballa, (the head center of will and purpose), with active engagement of the angelic and devic kingdoms. Also participating is the Mother of the world (the Being whose body is the substance of Earth or Gaia) and the Father of the world, (the Being who initiated the creation of the earth and holds it in manifestation), as well as galactic civilizations. Each planetary sphere of life has its own central focalizing presence, and are all held within the infinitely vast field of the Source/Creator whom we call God, the One Life or the Universe.

Shamballa, as an interplanetary center and council of will and purpose for the earth, is a major coordinating center for releasing energies for the next steps of the plan to the spiritual Masters and humanity. Each new movement forward requires a positive response from humanity, which is proceeding very well.

Each new release of energy or activating impulse is carefully considered by the Solar council and engaged galactic civilizations. The importance and significance of earth and humanity moving into higher dimensional understanding has invoked the full participation of all these levels of being and consciousness.

The energies to stimulate and support this unfoldment are being radiated in an unprecedented way from Shamballa, the Solar Logos, the center of the galaxy and the galactic civilizations. For this reason it is absolutely assured that the plan will be realized within the necessary timing, given the response now present within humanity.

The Coordination Process

When a new initiative is being prepared by the Solar Logos, everything is considered by the Solar council: the outline of the energies to be released; their frequency and intensity; the timing of the release; the dimensions and subplanes they are intended to affect; their likely impact on humanity; and the time it will take for their effects to be a anchored in the substance of humanity and the body of the earth. These are fully discussed and adjusted based on the highest wisdom of all the spiritual beings involved.

Once this is clarified, the timing for the release of the energies or stimulation is agreed upon. All forces then support and uphold this energetic release, and together work to maximize the positive effects and minimize the negative ones.

Uplifting the Middle East

There has been a long standing inner initiative, for example, to raise the energetic atmosphere in the Middle East to facilitate dialogue, create a reduction of hostilities based on ancient feuds, and establish a higher frequency field where positive initiatives could actually succeed. Meditation work is being done to purify and fill with light the mental, astral and etheric subplanes of this region through energetic cooperation with various angelic helpers.

A vortex has been created and anchored that is held open and energized by energies released by spiritual forces and human meditative teams. The energy flowing into this vortex is having a significant impact in the Middle East, and is one of the most important sources of transformational energy in the region.

All this inner work has been coordinated from the level of the Solar Logos and Shamballa, and the meditation work of members in small groups has contributed to this process of shifting conditions in the Middle East. And despite the serious conflicts necessary to burn way ancient karma, this will ultimately lead to positive initiatives for peace and reconciliation.

Other important sources are the many spiritual groups, interfaith initiatives, peace building efforts between cultures, and world prayers and meditations for peace in the region. The results of all these actions, including containment, meditation and the unfolding of events and exhaustion with war, is beginning a shift in attitudes and a new openness to positive approaches.

Chapter 8

Transformation of the World Financial System

One of the keys to unfolding the steps in the plan for transfiguration is a complete reform and reorganization of the world financial system. The current financial system was carefully designed by the dark lodge as the primary mechanism for controlling the planet and keeping humanity in fear and financial slavery for hundreds of years.

In the past years there has been a steadily accelerating exposure of the fraudulent, exploitive banking system, and the corrupt, interest-based currency issued by the Federal Reserve and other international banks that control and manipulate it.

There has been a major shift in personnel in many key financial institutions as more than 2000 top executives in major banks, financial exchanges and hedge funds have resigned, been indicted or committed suicide. This is all due to the influence of an organized light group, with representatives from many nations, that is working behind the scenes to transform the world financial system.

The Earth Light Alliance

A Light Alliance, reflecting the greater Galactic Light Alliance, was formed on earth as a result of decades of experience by world leaders with the cabal's brutal tactics and controlling manipulations of the world financial and political system. It is composed of uncompromised leaders worldwide who are dedicated to serving the best interests of humanity and who have seen firsthand the machinations and control of the cabal.

These lighted members of humanity, concerned about the well-being of earth and all life upon it, have been guided into a coordinated organization which is an earth-based extension of the Galactic Light Alliance. All members are working of their own free will in cooperation with the Galactic Alliance. This cooperation is consciously understood at many different levels by all participating.

The end result, however, is that there is a unified coordination of the Light Alliance that reaches from the Universal and Solar councils and the galactic civilizations through Shamballa, the spiritual Hierarchy and to humanity organized as the Earth Light Alliance. This is a unified energetic impulse which is unfolding the outworking of the plan on earth.

Evidence was provided to these world leaders of the cabal's under-ground bases (which were the size of cities, some holding up to 65,000 people), and their intended use as safe havens for the dark elites during an orchestrated nuclear war. They understood that the cabal's ultimate intent was to destroy and enslave humanity.

They also knew about the worldwide theft and appropriation of gold throughout history, with the goal of making printed money the only avail-able medium of exchange, which the cabal had achieved. These world financial and political leaders were familiar with the assassination and intimidation tactics of the cabal, and together agreed they must end this rule and establish a fair and workable financial system to stabilize the world economy and provide for the world's people.

Out of these agreements there emerged the consciousness for a major world reorganization of the financial system. The plan for reorganization of the world economy was co-created by humanity's lighted leaders and the greater Galactic Light Alliance, and it now has been carefully approved and is supported by most nations.

The Plan for Reorganizing the Financial System

The new financial plan has three major aspects:
- re-founding of the banking system under rigorous rules so banks serve the circulation of funds and promote fair exchange and eco-nomic activity;
- establishment of a new currency, backed by gold and other com-modities, issued by a completely trustworthy and impartial inter-national group to be formed;
- distribution of funds and resources to provide for the needs of every human being on the planet.

For a full unfolding of the higher plan to go forward, these financial and other changes must occur. The process of creating the conditions for all this to manifest is nearing completion, and it will be launched as soon as all factors are in place.

The Re-organization of Banks

Most of the major banks have been owned and operated by the cabal, and have been the main institutional control system for their power over the world. All banks will be re-chartered, with strict rules regarding their operations, including loans and all other functions.

There will be a fee for a loan, based on its size, but no interest will be charged for loans or for money put into circulation. The amount of money in the system will be carefully regulated to promote positive, balanced economic exchange.

Banks will not be profit-making companies, but rather will be run as public service utilities, like water, waste disposal, etc. Today, the controlling interest in major central banks in various countries is held by cabal families and groups, and this will be changed. Members of the general public with bank shares will be compensated as part of this reorganization.

Banks, Currencies and Investments

Each nation will have its own national bank to be used to regulate its economy. Each country will be able to print money as a national currency without interest, which will be convertible into the new international currency, available to all.

The forces of light are gaining control of the Bank of International Settlements, which is the capstone of the control system of international banking. Members of the cabal have been removed or turned from all positions of control over that system, and reform of the bank is beginning.

All banks will eventually be governed by boards of lighted economic experts who will carefully regulate them to maximize economic activity and the public good. There will also be local banks oriented towards serving the needs of people where they are located.

Most investments will retain their value, especially in positive companies contributing to the well-being of humanity. The shift to the new financial system will be orderly and everything will continue, except with different values and a new foundational financial system.

The New Currency

Although there will still be national currencies, the most significant will be the new worldwide currency, as it will be gold and commodity backed. The gold to back all this will come from what has been stolen and hidden by the cabal, as well as gold already held by the spiritual forces. All the vast wealth of the cabal will be taken and shared with the whole.

This new currency issued by the Alliance, backed by gold, will therefore have instant worldwide acceptance and credibility. There will be no interest attached to it, and its distribution will be guided by an international group from the Light Alliance.

Each national bank will issue the currency and credit for their nation. The present national currencies will be convertible into the new currency at a reasonable rate. The value of the exchange rate will be determined by the strength of each nation's economy, and the wisdom of its management, and will be verified by an international board. Eventually, national currencies will fade out.

Distribution of Funds to Humanity

There will be a worldwide distribution of funds and systems established to build earth- sensitive infrastructure to meet the basic needs of everyone in the world.

Immediate relief will be provided to those in greatest need, followed by the building of homes and sanitation, as well as providing health care, education and other needs for everyone.

People will be taught about their Divine essence and purpose, and helped to bring it into its fullest possible expression. The new system will be put in place internationally, not just in the United States, and the cabal will not be able to interfere in this.

Political Reforms to Allow Financial Transformation

The reform of the money system will also be part of a political reform, and those who have been aligned with the cabal will be removed and re-educated.

U.S. government shutdowns, debt and other crises were instigated by the cabal to create chaos, as they control the most divisive and polarized political groups. This crisis has seriously discredited these cabal forces within the Congress in the eyes of the public, and adds to the obvious need for major reform in people's minds. (As of August 2014, only 7% of the American people expressed confidence in the U.S. Congress.) This is a victory for the Light forces.

In the future, people will serve in government who care for the well-being of all those they represent, and no other agenda. Party affiliation will become less and less important, and ultimately fade out.

Some of the National Security Agency eavesdropping has been used by the Light Forces to gather information on the cabal and their activities. Charges will be brought against those who do not cooperate in establishing reforms in line with the spiritual plan.

There have been ongoing negotiations for years between the Light Alliance and the cabal, which has led to many members of the cabal turning to the light side. The issue of how past crimes will be handled has been part of the negotiations, as well as turning over all assets of the cabal, resigning from leadership positions, and turning over control of major institutions to the light forces.

The Timing of Major Changes on Our Planet

The timing of major financial and political changes is based on both cosmic factors and the co-creative efforts of humanity in instituting reforms and supporting new solutions that benefit the greater whole. For a full unfolding of the higher plan to go forward, these financial and other changes must occur.

Because free will and the readiness of human consciousness are key factors in implementing the Day of Revelation, the timing is not fixed. However, due to the plans and decrees of the Solar Being, the plan will be implemented within a reasonable time cycle for the well-being of humanity and the larger system.

The media will come under the control of the light forces at a carefully chosen time, and the international Light Alliance will introduce the new plan to the public through world media. The exact timing for the implementation of this plan is difficult to project, even for the higher spiritual forces. This is because it is such a complex operation, with such a vast number of factors (including human readiness) that must all be coordinated and brought together in a clear, culminating focus. It is far more complex than the D Day landing at Normandy in WWII, for example.

Also, a major factor in timing is the degree of cooperation with the plan by humanity, as we have free will, and if we choose, we can help speed up the process and thus avoid more suffering on the planet.

Even without more active human support, there is a certain solar systemic timing for the fulfillment of the plan which is not in the far distant future. But if we as humanity are more fully engaged in supporting the plan, major financial and political changes can be made more rapidly and more suffering can be eliminated.

Additional Evidence of the Unfolding Plan

- *Pope Francis* is one of the leaders of the Earth Light Alliance, and he is changing the spiritual tone of the Catholic Church and taking many practical steps to eliminate the corruption in the Vatican bank and its control, along with other banks, of the world financial system. The Pope is reorganizing the church bureaucracy, with each department now under the guidance and watchful eye of lighted leaders.

   He is also taking strong stands on the environment and climate change, and against slavery in all forms. Pope Francis's focus on global warming is based on guidance from the Light Alliance, and it is an important initiative to change humanity's consciousness about its relationship to earth and the nature kingdoms. During climate talks in Lima, Catholic bishops from every continent called for "an end to the fossil fuel era," as the impacts of a changing climate will disproportionately affect those who are least able to adapt (and who did not emit most of the pollution in the first place). Addressing the causes and effects of climate change is a moral and social justice issue for Catholics, along with prioritizing "the immediate needs of the most vulnerable communities," the bishops said.

The acceptance and open support of the Catholic Church for the upcoming financial and political reforms is a crucial part of the strategy to anchor these changes on the day of Revelation. Pope Francis is being overlighted by Master Jesus, St. Francis and other Masters. He has tremendous spiritual power flowing through him, and is able to transform much with his simple touch.

- *Reducing the nuclear threat*: Within two days during the week of October 7th, 2013, the U.S. Air Force general in charge of nuclear missiles, General Michael Carey, and the U.S. Naval Admiral with top nuclear weapons responsibilities, Vice Admiral Tim Giardina, were both fired. The threat of unleashing nuclear disaster on humanity has long been used by the cabal to stave off its final defeat by the light forces.

- *Chemical trail spraying* from airplanes, which was an attempt to downgrade human health through spraying harmful substances in the skies worldwide, is being reduced. Most importantly, the Galactics are neutralizing any harmful effects from these substances, as they have been charged, under the solar decree, with protecting humanity from any attempts by the cabal to compromise our health.

- *Over 2,000 CEOs or CFOs of banks, hedge fund managers, or top level financial executives have resigned*, been indicted or arrested, which is ten times the normal attrition rate.

- *An ever increasing number of whistleblowers* are coming forward and sharing information about corruption in every institution, resulting in many successful prosecutions.

- *The disbelief of a large percentage of people in the official explanations of 9/11* events, the Kennedy, King and many other assassinations, as well as the rationales given for bailouts of the corrupt banking system, and many other false stories about dark activities, is another example of public awakening.

- **The uprising of humanity against corruption and injustice** in many countries worldwide, such as Egypt, Libya and the Ukraine, is another indicator of the unfolding plan for transfiguration, as people demand freedom, equality and opportunity.

How We Can Each Play Our Part

It is absolutely essential for those of us who understand the significance of what is happening to hold this higher plan in our consciousness in every possible moment, seeing it coming to fruition and being fully realized on earth.

By doing this, we are using our will to help hold this plan as the future humanity is moving into, just as higher spiritual forces are also holding this for humanity. It is a plan which is being multi-dimensionally co-created, and it needs our fullest cooperation to anchor in the human dimension. Our intentions are extremely powerful in creating our reality.

It is important for other people to be informed about the nature of the unfolding plan, so that they can also stand, to the degree they are able, as points of clarity and understanding as the plan is revealed and unfolds.

Wherever we are, we can begin to seed human consciousness with ideas from the plan that can be received by those we are informally in contact with. We can also present these ideas in articles and talks and in other ways people can accept.

We can meditate individually and in groups and project lighted thoughts about this vision for humanity's positive future into the mental field of humanity.

We can endeavor to live in a continuous state of love and joyful expectancy as much as possible, practicing gratitude for our life and the opportunities of this momentous time.

We can continue to trust that the higher Powers are profoundly orchestrating this entire transfiguration process, and all is moving forward for the highest good of all.

Meditation on Light

1. Meditate on light and its emergence from the point of light within the mind of Source/God. Sense that light, see it, feel its vibration, and sense the quickening of your energy and frequencies from its presence.

2. Become aware of that pure light within you, focusing on that light, but not on what the light may reveal to you.

3. Stay within this light, immerse yourself in it, feel its radiance and upliftment, its presence deep within your being, not in any particular location, but simply omnipresent within you. Recognize this light is the same light within the Divine Source. Stay within this light for several minutes.

4. Now sense the light's effect on your chakra energy system, and where it is most perceptible as an increased frequency, a quickening of your energies. Allow this light to fully radiate through your entire being, sensing which chakras are most infused with it, which ones are less so.

5. See this light radiating gently through all your chakras, clearing, purifying and irradiating them. See your atoms being irradiated, and see your DNA spirals being filled with light and returning to their true configuration to allow you full consciousness in all dimensions.

6. Now, remembering the truth that "within the light all is light," focus your attention on the earth and see if you can perceive, at the very core of the earth, the light within it. Recognize that this light is the same light substance found within all forms on all levels, from an atom to solar system.

7. See the light within the heart core of the earth increasing in brightness, radiating and filling the entire earth and all life upon it with light.

Section III

Free Will and the Light Alliance

Chapter 9

The Nature and Significance of Free Will in Creation

The will as a faculty of the human being has been widely misunderstood. It is usually viewed as the exercise of force or effort, an intense focusing of attention and energy to achieve a specific outcome, a state of consciousness or state of being. It has also generally been interpreted as the expression of the dynamic, active, masculine polarity. The will can be used and applied in this manner, but this is not its fullest or highest expression.

Will, in its deepest essence, is at the heart of what makes humanity Divine. In the process of using the will, and the functions of choice, intention, focusing, attracting, assembling and organizing elements of any creation on any level, humanity is functioning in resonance with the Divine pattern of the creative process. Thus, all willed creation is a spiritual act, expressing our essential Divine nature.

The Creator allows all forms of creation, positive or negative, benevolent or harmful, for the resulting learning and ultimate evolution of consciousness and growth of the soul. The human soul also allows negative creations, and the lessons learned are absorbed by the soul, guaranteeing better future choices.

Thus free will is the Divine birthright of every human being, and marks the entrance into a portal distinct from the animal kingdom. What distinguishes human free will is the freedom to create.

The Significance of Free Will

The living heart of any creation is the choice of what, where and how to create made by its creator. Free will is the circulating energy from the heart which brings things into being. Free will, granted by the Creator as a gift to humanity, is known throughout all the cosmos as a great, expansive pulse of joyous creation.

Creation is Divine when it is expressed in harmony with all lives in all systems, based on love and lighted understanding of the whole, and intending enhancement and freedom for all. All factors, beings and dimensions are given their rightful place and function within the vision and plan of this type of higher order creator.

This is the ensouling pattern held by the Creator of the earth, the solar system and the seven solar systems.

It is also reflected in powerful human acts of spiritual co-creation on earth, such as the Magna Carta, the Declaration of Independence, the Universal Declaration of Human Rights, and all great franchises of freedom won through human and Divine co-creation.

Free will can only be understood within a true field of freedom to use Divine power to create, and to make any possible choice. And through experience, we finally realize the truth that the highest use of our will is to create conditions and possibilities that allow the greatest freedom and growth for all.

Because of the Divine and cosmic nature of free will found within every human being, any attempt to curtail, control or manipulate the free will of others is eventually doomed to failure. This is the foundational truth upon which the inevitable breakdown and dissolution of the dark lodge on earth rests.

Free will is sacred and Divine and nothing can stop its gaining full expression by the sacred Ruler who abides in every human heart. This provides an understanding of why the spiritual Masters give such significance to free will as an inviolable principle.

All assistance now being given to humanity is a result of the freely chosen cry for freedom from the heart of humanity, and the focused intention of conscious servers to liberate humanity into the freedom of our Divine birthright. We are very close to achieving this realization of our essential human/Divine nature.

From this foundation, humanity is learning the right use of the will and its many functions. It is central to the creative process, not just in its active aspect of synthesizing all that is required, but also in its receptive, nurturing, space-holding capacity — keeping the intention clear while allowing the process to unfold.

Human Free Will and the Plan

You may ask whether a higher plan is an imposition upon the free will of humanity. The answer is that the full play and outworking of human free will and choice is a core principle of the plan. This has been allowed, despite all the harm and suffering resulting from these choices. However, when the expression of free will threatens the existence of the planet itself, and holds back the evolution of higher beings such as our entire solar system, then higher Powers have the right to intervene and correct the situation.

They are doing this by guiding humanity into a wider field of life through the transfiguration process, and allowing each individual to make their free will choice to enter the matrix of love or not. Those who cannot live in this high energetic frequency and are not ready for this evolutionary step will be lovingly removed from earth. This is being done to provide those not yet ready with a safe haven to continue their growth in a system suited to their level of development. Thus, the plan offers free will as well as the creation and maintenance of environments allowing the maximum spiritual growth for all.

The Higher Functions of the Will

The higher functions of the will have to do with the transcendence of time within the creative process. The will provides the capacity to work both within and outside of time simultaneously. Within the dimensions of time, the will organizes the fulfillment of the intended creation by holding the intention, sounding the note of creative purpose, and attracting all the necessary elements to the chosen location in time and space.

The will, combined with vision, provides the template within which all is related and ordered. It infuses the creation with life force to allow its growth and unfoldment, while holding space for the optimum development of the energetic matrix of the new form. It then allows its crystallization and liberation from form when its cycle is completed.

The will also functions outside the realm of time by seeing a vast field of relationships, within which the contemplated creation will be born. It is used by the Divine Presence within each of us to hold the intent for the highest possible benevolent effects within the larger matrix of love and light.

The will is used as a synthetic faculty, to perceive the end from the beginning of the creation, so that all possible outcomes are understood. This includes recognizing the random unknown factors of the free will choices of all those engaged with the creation.

Thus free will is allowed within an intended, carefully held creation, even as choices are allowed to be made which can subvert the original intent of the creator. Thus the sacred principle of free will is upheld in all dimensions and worlds and is supported in all conditions.

Every act of human creation, no matter how simple or distorted, is like the first step of a child walking the path into becoming a fully realized Divine creator. The process begins with the willed creation of a form, and the perfecting of that created form, with humanity ultimately learning how to become the creator of vast worlds.

The growth into Divine creation has no end nor limit, only those self-created limitations by each human center of consciousness, which endlessly expand, as consciousness unfolds into its full understanding and glory as the One. Yet each center retains the capacity for creation in its self-chosen sphere, while aware of its oneness with All, the One Life.

One of the most important uses of our creative will at this time in history is to avoid allowing ourselves to be hypnotized into believing the chaotic, dark reality being projected by the cabal-controlled media. Instead we can maintain our focus on supporting the plan unfolding in the light of higher, spiritual reality.

(See end of Section III for a meditation on the Will in Creation).

Chapter 10

The Light Alliance and the Day of Revelation

The Light Alliance

Currently, many major nations are members of the earth dimension of the Light Alliance, and the interests of the smaller nations are also part of the plan. These major nations have agreed to support the higher plan. Some have reservations about its feasibility, but they are willing to support it in general because of its positive intent.

The human leaders of the Earth Light Alliance are awakened heads of state of major nations, and leaders in other fields of human endeavor. They are being advised by spiritually advanced members of the Galactic Light Alliance, including both members of earth's spiritual hierarchy and the Galactics.

These leaders are being advised, either through receiving inspiration and ideas through their inner process or through direct contact with "advisors." They may or may not realize these advisors are actually Masters, initiates or galactic helpers.

Thus the Galactics are assisting in three important ways. They are protecting earth from any outside interference by harmful nonhuman races, which will never happen again; they are blocking any moves by the cabal to damage earth or humanity in any major operations; and they are advising earth members of the Light Alliance.

The Light Alliance has been strengthened by the working relationships between members that have developed as the action plans have become more specific, and greater and greater trust is being built among all the members.

All is being very carefully planned and orchestrated so that the revelatory shift will be universal, seamless, and easily accepted by people of earth. Timing is determined by a very large number of factors, and the remaining resistances on earth are not major ones.

The core factors include energetic astrological alignments, the final preparation and readiness of new systems to be put into place, and the openness and demand of humanity for deep, real transformation in the world. This final factor, most admirably, is very strong at this time. The Galactic Light Alliance, at the highest spiritual levels, as well as the heads of nations and institutions as the Earth Light Alliance, will together implement the plan.

It is an integral part of the plan that the millions of good people in the world will widely and actively help this process, once the underlying plan is clear and institutional structures are reformed. The Light Alliance is confident this will occur, as so many are already engaged in reforms and innovative solutions to problems, even within the current corrupted system.

The political changes and removal of corrupt individuals from the U.S. Congress will happen simultaneously with the economic reforms. The reformed judicial branch, with the backing of the military, will use evidence of the cabal's activities collected by NSA. This agency is now largely under the control of the light forces, and its true purpose will be revealed very soon. This will be a shock to many who were uncomfortable with the loss of privacy, and it will take time for all this to be absorbed by the public consciousness.

Those who fund many retrogressive initiatives are major leaders of the cabal, as are those directing some major financial institutions. All these will be removed and their strongholds purified as the plan unfolds.

This is why it is necessary and valuable for people to be informed about the unfolding plan, so those who understand it can educate others as to the underlying causes and true motives of those leading these changes.

The Day of Revelation of the Plan

The higher spiritual Forces call the moment when the plan is implemented and announced publicly the Day of Revelation. The spiritual Masters will not announce their involvement at that time, but at a later point they will. The Galactics' presence and role will also be disclosed some time later. The exact timing depends on the response of humanity to these events.

On the Day of Revelation there will be a worldwide holiday and announcements will be made from a central location, possibly at the United Nations or another site. This is unresolved because there is a struggle ongoing within the UN between the forces of light and darkness, and there is also mistrust of the UN by many people because of its past mistakes, and the attacks on it by the cabal.

At the moment of the announcement, all actions needed to implement the changes will already be underway. This will include changing the banking system, and arresting some politicians and other corrupt leaders and officials.

After a short period when all systems are closed, the entire world financial system will reopen on the new financial basis outlined earlier, with all interest based money, financial derivatives and other corrupt banking practices eliminated. All is intended to be as seamless as possible, with a minimum of disruptions, and this is likely to be the case.

It is not expected that there will be any major paranoid reaction to the financial reorganization once the terms of the new system are announced and people see its benevolent intent.

Those who are aware of the plan can be talking about it with others in advance if there is openness and opportunity. Once the Revelation of the plan begins, it will be the time for full sharing of all that we, as light workers, understand.

The Arrest of Key Figures

There was a period in negotiations with the cabal when it appeared it might be possible to reach an agreement for them to step down, relinquish all power systems, and allow trained Light Alliance members to assume control.

However, due to their intransigence, this was not possible. The plan now is to arrest and indict those responsible, remove them from power, and allow the Light Alliance to begin to implement the plan, having full control or cooperation from those leaders remaining.

There will be indictments handed down for bribery, corruption, malfeasance and all manner of betrayals of office. These will be served and the accused taken into custody. Members from both political parties in the U.S. will be arrested. Once the nature of the indictments are revealed, a proceeding will remove them from continuing to serve in Congress and other government agencies.

In the meantime, the executive, judicial and military will be in charge, although some Supreme Court and other justices will be removed.

Certain corporate executives will also be indicted and arrested, as they are deeply involved with the cabal and many are leaders of it. The military will be involved with the process of removing cabal members, if necessary, as a high percentage of military officers are now positively oriented to the plan, at various levels.

This may all seem fantastical given the current world situation, yet a true paradigm shift is always disruptive of the old. This entire plan is emphatically and strongly supported by the Solar council, the spiritual governing body of our Solar system, and the Universal council.

The same type of cleanout will be done in other countries on the same day. It will be a Revelation of the true intent of the plan and the Light Alliance, which is worldwide.

This Day of Revelation is a specific moment when all is put into motion, and when what was hidden is revealed. The karmic scales are weighed and correct action, supported by higher spiritual Powers, is taken to bring the planet into full resonance and conscious understanding of its true history and its place within the Alliance of Light.

What is being created by these spiritual powers cannot be blocked, resisted or subverted. These powers have given us their solemn vow that this is so. It will be the single most important date in the history of the world.

Chapter 11

The Cabal's Loss of Power

Although there are not many outer indications of what is occurring and shifting under the surface, massive changes in the power dynamics in the world have already occurred. The cabal is losing control of the central banking system, which is gradually being managed by the light forces.

The cabal's control of the political system is also fading as the more fanatical conservative elements have been further discredited because of the damage to the economy from their extreme pro-wealthy, anti-middle class approach. People from all sectors, are beginning to see their true colors and are turning against them.

The inner changes have not yet fully manifested outwardly in the political and financial arenas because everything has to be organized, prepared and implemented worldwide in a coordinated, powerful action. This is already well planned, and will occur when all the timing factors are in place.

The cabal remnants are only able to create negative events on a very minor scale and these will be quickly controlled. All the random mass shootings by individuals who have been mentally programmed will be stopped. There are small, negative groups causing pockets of resistance in various locations, but they are not fundamentally delaying the unfoldment of the plan, as none of these are significant, and are not part of the world control systems.

How has the cabal been able to do all the harmful things it has and not experience rebounding karma, with huge negative results? The negative effects are very present in the spiritual impact of their activities, leading to their isolation, guilt, fear, etc. There are also karmic effects like accidents and disease.

The cabal wanted to rule openly, which is why they launched the 9/11 attacks to begin a process to reduce the world's population. Their plan was to use the fear of terrorists to reduce human freedoms and instigate nuclear war in the Middle East. They wanted to be known and revered publicly so they would receive life energy from people knowing about them and focusing on them. Their deep sense of guilt and unworthiness sought relief in such a dynamic.

But they did not dare to rule openly until they completely controlled the world with a reduced population, which they did not, and will not, ever achieve. All this has been brought down and they are losing power each day that passes. Their karma will soon come back to them as the higher plan is brought into full manifestation.

Economic Reforms

The financial reforms are moving steadily forward and all is on track. There has been a strengthening and clarifying of the international Earth Light Alliance in preparation for the reorganization of the financial system, including debt forgiveness.

Positively oriented groups and individuals in the United States are cooperating with this higher plan for financial reorganization. There is enough support in the U.S., including within the military, to turn the tide for reform.

Developments in the Media

The WikiLeaks exposure of the details of the Trans Pacific Partnership negotiations, showing the proposed agreement would only give more power to corporations and eliminate environmental and other protections, was an action of the light forces. It was only reported in the alternative press, and did not emerge in the mainstream press because it was suppressed by the cabal. However, this will shift soon, and all will be seen in its true light as the plan is revealed.

Control of the media is one of the final holdout areas, and will be the last to fall, as the cabal knows when this is lost, they are finished. There is currently prosecution of some media corruption and reorganizing of many media outlets underway to bring them into the hands of light workers, as has happened with the Washington Post. The trial of the editors of Rupert Murdoch's London papers is another example of this. Much of this is happening below public awareness and reporting, but the signs are there, as lies and manipulations of the public by the media are being exposed.

Middle East Peace

Various nations and factions are gradually exhausting themselves in war, and now is the time when peace initiatives in the Middle East can make some progress. The interim agreement between Iran and the U.S. and five other world powers is a key step in building trust and developing a resolution of the nuclear issue with Iran. This is a complete reversal of the cabal's effort to stimulate conflict with Iran, and an important step in creating conditions in the world for further unfolding of the plan.

Signs of the Upheaval in the Natural World

There is tremendous pressure everywhere in the world at this time, due to the energies present and the central struggle between the Light Alliance and the cabal, which is an extremely intense process.

There are always disasters when the inner planes are such a battleground. The typhoon in the Philippines was an expression in the natural world of the inner storms raging. This event was also a karmic outworking of Atlantean patterns with groups who supported the dark lodge during that ancient period, leading to the destruction of Atlantis by natural disaster, just as their world has been devastated today. The outpouring of love and the donations from the hearts of people around the world is helping to transmute this ancient karma.

Tornados in the American Midwest, new volcanic eruptions, and other intense weather patterns such as earthquakes and floods, are all part of the natural purification process of the earth, as it shakes off the negative energies which have been predominant for so long.

Chapter 12

Signs of the Plan
in the Mainstream Media

Financial Karma – Negative and Positive

- *J.P. Morgan* paid a $13 billion settlement for knowingly selling bad loans packaged as securities to unwitting investors, including federal and state agencies — the largest settlement ever between government and a single company.

- *Currency traders* at some of the world's biggest banks, such as Citibank, Barclays, JP Morgan and UBS, are being investigated by international officials for rigging the $5.3 trillion a day foreign exchange market, with major fines being levied against them.

- *The Dutch lender Rabobank* agreed to pay more than $1 billion in criminal and civil penalties from manipulation of the Libor interest rates, and the chief executive has resigned.

- *Many U.S. and European banks still face years of effort and billions of dollars in legal charges*, The New York Times reported, including Deutsche Bank of Germany, UBS in Switzerland, Lloyds and Barclays of London. Many are being investigated   simultaneously by regulators from the U.S., Switzerland, Britain, Germany and many other countries.

- *Costa Rica's banks have been publicly owned* by mutual associations, credit unions and the national government for the last 64 years, in spite of enormous pressure by the IMF to privatize them. These public banks have not failed in 31 years and 80% of all retail deposits in Costa Rica are held by the top four government owned banks, who finance the private sector. Costa Rica has not been affected by ups and downs in the world economy because local businesses can get money when they need it, which is set by government policy.

- *Occupy Wall Street activists* have bought a small part of American's personal debt as part of the Rolling Jubilee project to help people pay off their outstanding medical debts. The $15 million in debts that was retired was purchased by the activists at a discount from banks at a cost of $400,000, with the funds raised from donations averaging $40.

Political Signs

- *Xi Jinping, President of China*, has assumed the role of change agent, after a leadership meeting of the Communist Party, and announced new policies easing restrictions on the one child family, abolishing reeducation through labor camps, moving the economy away from highly polluting industries, and relaxing restrictions on land ownership and state control of interest rates, and vigorously going after corrupt officials.

- *The U.S. and China have been cooperating on reducing greenhouse gases.* Driven by domestic demands and not wanting to be seen as the world's super polluters, they have formed a working group to help speed action on climate change.

- *Three women Senators*, supported by 17 other women Senators in the U.S. Congress, took a leading role in proposing a solution to the polarized deadlock about government spending which had temporarily closed the U.S. government. This enabled the government to reopen and averted a financial default.

Galactic Views

A Huff Post/YouGov poll revealed that *48% of adults in the U.S. are open to the idea that ET spacecraft are observing our planet*—and only 35% outright reject the idea.

Astronomers at University of California, Berkeley have calculated that there at least *50 billion stars much like earth's sun.* They estimate that 11 billion planets about the size of earth are orbiting around these suns, at a distance that make temperatures there possible for liquid water to exist, and providing potential conditions for human life.

Reflection and Meditation on the Will in Creation

The will, balanced within the matrix of love, and infused with light, is utilized at every step in the process of creation. It can be useful to the plan to choose something positive which you wish to create — a state of consciousness, a new attitude or habit, a change in a relationship, a reorganization of your life for a new purpose, or a project you wish to create as a gift to the world.

Remember that the plan is made up of billions of positive, light oriented choices by humanity, so it does not need to be a huge project. A positive change in an attitude or a relationship is a contribution to the plan for transfiguration.

You can view your intended creation as an application of your will,

---

aligned with Divine Will, infused with light and manifested within the matrix of love. You can reflect on your choice of what you would like to create with these questions:

1. What is the purpose of this creation? What or who is it serving? How does it align within the plan for the transfiguration of the world? Does it need adjustment?

2. Now visualize the end from the beginning, seeing clearly what the outcome of this creation can be. Then use your will to hold this outcome clearly throughout the entire creative process. Recognize that many factors will influence the actual result, yet hold a positive outcome nonetheless.

3. Infuse the purpose of your creation with light and intelligence, assessing how light, new awareness and greater freedom for all will flow from this creation.

4. Open to the matrix of love, allowing your purpose and will to be infused with love and resonate with love, being fully unfolded within it, to protect it from distorted types of creations.

5. See the attraction of all the energies, people and resources needed to allow your creation to come into being in the mental, emotional and etheric/physical dimensions. Allow for unexpected help, synchronicities and serendipitous events to occur to assist in this co-creation.

6. Materialize the creation into full magnificence in the worlds of form by seeing it emerging first on the mental level as a clear thought form, then emotionally charged with positive enthusiasm and attraction, and then appearing on the physical dimensions.

7. Nurture this creation with your life force, knowing it will grow and unfold into its full, true beauty.

8. Detach yourself from your creation, and allow it to fulfill its intended purpose, Within right timing, withdraw your life energy and allow it to dissolve into its elements, to be re-created again in a new form.

The Cycles of Civilization and The Day of Revelation

Chapter 13

The Media Façade,
and Our Role as Free Agents

The struggle with the dark cabal is nearly over. Their resistance is broken, and they are scattering and deeply divided among themselves. They know the end of their reign is approaching, and they are deeply fearful of what is to come. The top leaders of the cabal are also aware that the spiritual powers are preparing to move against them.

The goal of the cabal-controlled media is to keep up the façade that all is continuing under the current controllers, and everything is normal. With the Day of Revelation, this façade will crumble, and the truth will be revealed. Underneath, there are massive shifts occurring which are destabilizing their rule. They are losing control of the money system, the masses are revolting, and more information is coming out every day about their systems of control and manipulation.

In the past year there have been protest demonstrations around all types of issues in 34 countries, many focused on the financial system and the control by the wealthiest 1%, and the unmet needs of many of the other 99% of people.

Those who are choosing to move in anti-evolutionary directions, towards separation, violence and all manner of anti-life attitudes and actions, have been given every opportunity to turn from such patterns towards the light of love and the human community.

The Light Alliance is not expecting major shifts in the leadership choices of the cabal, although negotiations are ongoing to some degree. The die has been cast on who will be removed from the earth and who will not. The time is fast approaching when all those immersed in darkness will no longer have free reign on the planet, but will, in fact, be placed in situations where they can do no more harm to the whole.

For some this means arrest, imprisonment and being held accountable for their actions. For others, it is removal to another planetary system in keeping with their vibrational frequency, where they can continue to evolve in an environment more appropriate for them. This is, in fact, the most loving action that can be taken, as it prevents them from continuing to harm others and accruing further karmic debts, and thus prolonging their suffering.

Parting of the Ways

This great reorganization of the planetary life will take time to fully implement, and it will cut through and across families, organizations, and nations.

As this occurs, it is essential to understand and remember that a great benevolent higher Power is behind all that unfolds — a Power whose only intent is the highest good of every life form, every atom of substance in the entire planetary, and ultimately, solar systemic life.

This benevolent higher Power will continue to support all who are removed from society, and are taken into other planetary systems that offer opportunities to redirect their steps towards the light.

This perspective is being given to help knowers of the plan provide a deeper understanding to others of what is occurring on the planet, and offer a positive, benevolent context to unfolding events. These are always proceeding within the matrix of love, without exception.

Our Role as Free Agents in the New Earth

Each individual soul incarnated on the planet at this time is present for a specific reason. It may be to heal a relationship, complete some karma, learn a particular lesson, or fulfill a purpose which contributes to a group, nation or the world. The unfolding of the plan consists of the embodied fulfillment of the soul purposes of each of these billions of lives, moving forward into greater light, love and empowerment.

For all those who remain free agents on planet earth, our task will be reorganizing and rebuilding life on earth in harmony with the Divine cosmic order.

This means that the spiritual, mental, emotional and etheric/physical well-being of every life form on the planet is the priority of the Divine order being established. Every decision and every plan for human and natural life will be approached within this higher pattern.

Not only does the goal of providing shelter, food, healthcare, clothing, education and creative opportunities for every human being become the great, joyful work, but everyone's choices and participation in the design of these programs will be essential.

This will honor the Divine essence within each person, and allow them to exercise their Divine right as creators of their lives and world.

Our Service Contributions

Each of us all over the world can become fully aware and informed focal points of light to help in the implementation of the plan. Knowing the deep background and history of earth, and the interaction of the forces of light and darkness, can give you the confidence and understanding to stand more powerfully for the plan wherever you are.

A very important dimension of your service contribution is in the world of thought. By focusing on the deeper, underlying patterns and plans that are being carried forward on earth, and adding your thought energy, joyful anticipation, love, and sense of purpose, you are building a major group center through which the plan can be magnified.

Because many of us are trained and experienced meditators, these skills can contribute mightily to the unfolding plan. Every fully informed light worker who knows why and how the plan is being unfolded is a knower of the plan who is helping to co-create its emergence.

This is the purpose of this series of transmissions and why this information is now being revealed — to empower, inspire, and energize people, and to give strength, vision and courage to every light worker.

You then can take your rightful place and stand with the great interplanetary Alliance of Light, contributing your energy, thought and deep love in support of this great revelation and transformation.

Each individual will know what he or she can do and how best to contribute — through thought and meditation, sharing appropriate information with those who are receptive, and organizing gatherings to help people understand what is underway on our beloved planet earth.

Chapter 14

The Cycles of Civilizations

In the history of the unfoldment of the plan, there have been times when a major shift in consciousness and in the world order has been possible. These have occurred when a civilization has reached the peak of its development and expression, and is about to enter a cycle of decline and decay.

It is at these unique times in the life cycle of a civilization that an opportunity is available to reorient, renew and rebirth the civilization. Now is such a moment in the history of our world.

However, this moment of reorientation and rebirth of earth is unique because of all the factors we are exploring: the culmination of the struggle between the forces of light and dark; the great decrees of the Universal and Solar councils; the engagement and aid of the galactic civilizations; and the inpouring of light and love to the earth through its alignment with the center of the galaxy. This alignment is a source point for many of the powerful energies stimulating our earth at this time. All of these factors guarantee a complete and successful rebirth for all life on earth.

In addition, the mass spiritual awakening occurring among people in every nation on earth, despite all the efforts of the dark lodge to prevent it, magnifies the opportunity and guarantees success.

Because of the inflowing light and love as well as modern telecommunications, never before in the history of the world has the entire population been so enlivened and awakened, so aware of its fundamental unity across all barriers of nations, cultures, race and religion, despite all efforts to stimulate fear and separateness.

Because of all these factors and conditions, the unprecedented elevation of our civilization and the ascension of human consciousness are occurring.

This shift on earth will ripple throughout the galaxy, as within the unified field of the matrix of love, any shift in any part of the field affects the whole.

The transformational shift of a planetary body that is a chakra in the greater body of the Solar Logos is an especially stupendous event. It is one that the spiritual hierarchy has foreseen, planned and worked towards for millions of years. It has been known that it would resonate through the cosmic field beyond our solar system into the galaxy. The exact extent of the emanation is not precisely known, but it will have effects throughout the entire unified field.

Clearing the Debris of the Old Civilization

A major part of the plan is clearing the debris of the old civilization from the consciousness of humanity on the mental, emotional and etheric/physical planes, much of which has been created and energized by the dark lodge.

Humanity has allowed its consciousness and life force to be used to feed these dark and distorted images of what it means to be human, believing that people can live successfully while violating all laws of love, life and the universe.

The extremes of religion, political ideologies, wealth, control, and media frenzies are running rampant in human civilization at this time. This reveals the complete illogic, uselessness and harm to all life on our planet from the current system. It provides a clear opening for the new systems, as the evil will soon have burned itself out and faced its karmic collapse. Then the public will be open and ready for a new, higher approach to human living.

These old patterns of thought and emotion are steadily being cleared and purified as light permeates the deeper and darker strata of each sub-plane. Purifying and withdrawing your attention and that of other people's from these dark, outmoded and dying patterns of thought, feeling and action is as important as creating a vision of the new world.

This is done by nonparticipation in all that is of the heavier, lower vibrations, such as fear, hate, greed and manipulation, and shifting instead to what is energized within the matrix of love.

A true spiritual warrior's practice of vigilance is essential: developing the practice of evaluating the moment-to-moment use of your attention and what you are feeding energy into.

You then can make a free will choice to not attend to all that is dark and harmful and keeps consciousness bound in lower frequencies, but instead focus on the unfolding plan.

At any moment when your consciousness is influenced by the darker energies, you can refocus on the beauty, joy and upliftment found in living within the plan of transfiguration for our world, which is your pathway of liberation.

Each and every one of us can help all those we communicate with in any way to lift their consciousness into the creative possibilities within the light, and out of the darkness and chains of the old civilization.

Simply being fully present and radiating through your thought and presence all the good you know is underway is a subtle communication that has a major effect on others. This practice raises your consciousness, makes you a conscious co-creator with the Alliance of Light, and also makes a major contribution to catalyzing the unfolding plan.

Chapter 15

The Day of Revelation
and the Regeneration of Earth

Another central pillar of the plan is the well-being and freedom of all members of the nature kingdoms to live out their lives within the life of the Divine Mother.

The kingdoms of nature are meant to be an acknowledged part of the Divine community of the One Life. The relationship between all life forms and humanity will take on a new dimension as the energy flowing within and between all life forms becomes visible to many humans.

This etheric life energy field, which surrounds and interpenetrates every life form, will be seen by approximately 20% of humanity. The validation of large numbers of people reporting what they see, will revolutionize scientific, social and interpersonal understanding. It will release a wave of new consciousness which will permeate human awareness, stimulating more and more people to open to this perception.

This is a step towards the ascension of human consciousness to perceive the fourth and fifth dimensions. It will be stimulated by the energies released on the Day of Revelation and the removal of the dark veils.

This will transform the relationships with all kingdoms of life into an experience of the universal beloved community of earth, living harmoniously in joyous, playful relationship.

Changes After the Day of Revelation

Many people see the Day of Revelation, which they call "The Event," as humanity moving into the fourth and fifth dimensions, but they do not pay much attention to what will happen outwardly in the world or within their own internal energy system.

However, many people will have a major shift inwardly in consciousness into higher dimensions, and for most, there will be a release of fear, which will allow a new openness to love. Huge amounts of love are flooding the earth now, and this will increase and intensify around the Day of Revelation.

The regeneration of the earth, humanity and nature will begin very soon after the Day of Revelation due to the accompanying installation of new financial and political systems, which will allow us to attend to the many issues that require immediate, loving attention. Plans are already in place for the construction of millions of new types of energy-efficient dwellings which can be created very quickly, using existing technologies.

New ways of accessing clean water will be introduced, and energy systems using free energy, which draw energy directly from the etheric planes, will be rapidly put in place. With this energy, desalinization plants can be built rapidly and pure water made available to all.

More healthy food will be grown in local communities all over the planet, and for the one billion people engaged in agriculture, working in harmony with the earth will become a joyful and creative pursuit.

New types of healthcare and health maintenance will be put in place. Clean, non-polluting forms of transportation will be established. Before full disclosure of their existence, the Galactics will provide some new technologies, to help humanity understand the benefits that the Galactics bring.

Releasing Subconscious Survival Fears

Once a sense of safety, security and well-being is established, many of the unresolved subconscious issues within humanity will be lessened in their intensity.

Classes will be established in every country to help people understand their own nature, how to improve themselves, grow spiritually, and become happier and more productive contributors to the whole.

Without the resistance and sabotage of this educational process by the cabal, it will spread very rapidly, and greatly enhance the joy, cooperation and co-creation of people everywhere.

Once the fear of scarcity and the threat of competition are reduced and then eliminated, international relations will become a field of enjoyable exchanges, travel and learning.

People will experience and enjoy the vast diversity of cultures, traditions, art, music, dance and folkways that are found on earth. Relationships will become a field of loving communion and wonderful creativity, improving the life and well-being of the whole world.

Unfolding Stages of the Plan

Although it is near, we are not yet at the culminating point when all major changes will be launched, and dramatic revelations made. The exact moment depends on readiness of all plans and personnel, as well decrees from the highest councils of light. The forces of light know there is a necessary timing which cannot be postponed, and this is the basis for all anticipation.

The unfolding of events begins with the Day of Revelation of the truth about earth's hidden history, accompanied by the financial and political changes; next there will be disclosure of the galactic civilizations; then ascension into higher consciousness by humanity will begin; and finally there will be the physical appearance of the spiritual Masters on earth.

Many people will ascend into higher consciousness during this period. All we each need to do is continue with our service and growth into greater love and joy, while holding the clear intention that this new world will manifest as we meditate on this vision and share what we know.

Chapter 16

Financial Changes on the Day of Revelation

The world financial system will be closed down for some days during the Day of Revelation. People need to be psychologically prepared for this and help others not to be in fear.

During this time, the financial system will be reset on a new basis as described earlier. No legitimately gained resources will be lost. All those who have acquired money and property through illegitimate means will have it confiscated. All this wealth will be returned to the whole.

Offices will be set up where legitimate claims can be filed for restitution of the deprivations and confiscations due to the cabal's manipulations of the financial system. There will be people present who can psychically determine if someone is placing a false claim. There will be consequences for doing so, and all will know this screening will be in place. Consequently there will be little fraud. Claims will include mortgage and rent payments for personal homes, but not for businesses, and there will be limits on the amounts to be refunded to each person.

All goods and services will then be priced based on their true value, without the inflated cost of borrowing money and paying interest. This will lower prices substantially, while placing adequate funds in the hands of the people of the world, and result in the rapid creation of prosperity for all.

There are well known business and political figures who are part of the Light Alliance. Some of them are simply aligned with the light, and others, depending on their need to know, depth of inquiry and capacity to hold the knowledge, are fully aware of the plan.

The Environmental Prime Directive

An environmental ethic and prime directive will be instituted in all financial and business transactions, and this will be applied worldwide. No financial or business activity will be permitted which does not give first priority to the ecological health and well-being of living beings and systems on the planet. This alone will radically transform all life on the planet.

The weather will be balanced and moderated and the intensive storms will cease, as the negative energies in certain locations which upheavals have released will have been cleared from the planet.

Free energy from the etheric planes will be introduced after the Day of Revelation using galactic technologies. People will know it is from the Galactics, and this will be part of how humanity will be prepared to accept this contact as completely benevolent. It will also be revealed to humanity that the Galactics have supported the shift leading up to the Day of Revelation.

The Rejuvenation Process

After the Day of Revelation and a longer period of adjustment into higher consciousness by humanity and our social systems, we will have disclosure of the Galactics, when the process of rejuvenation will become available to humanity. There are devices of the Galactics which can rejuvenate and restore the active functioning of DNA by providing a renewed and purified connection to the etheric field which sustains it.

This repairs, renews and revitalizes the DNA, which then stimulates all atoms in the body to a higher frequency vibration. From this shift, all cells, organs and systems within the body are given new life and energy to naturally renew themselves.

This technology will be universally available to humanity, once the reordering of the world is completed and disclosure is accomplished. This will make the Galactics universally welcomed. Earth will no longer be a vale of tears and suffering, but will be a planet of joy, and its song will rise throughout the heavens.

Visualizing Our Unfolding Future World

- Make an alignment with your highest source of spiritual light, love and power.

- Choose a field of human life that you resonate with, such as politics, business, education, healing, the arts, science, etc. Begin to reflect on and visualize how this area of human life could unfold if the influence of the dark lodge were completely eliminated, and humanity was living within the matrix of love and light. Visualize humanity using its creative will in that specific field.

- Allow the full play of your imagination, and do not be bound by what currently exists. Carry this out with the clear intention and full understanding that you are making a major creative contribution to the new world by imagining this beautiful future. You are functioning as a Divine creator, helping to sculpt and build the new world, through the power of your thought, infused with your love of the One Life.

- Pause and allow time for these ideas, visions and joyful possibilities to be fully absorbed and then record them.

- Later they can be shared with others, stimulating people with new visions, and seeding the thought field of humanity with creative possibilities.

- Such an exercise is using your creative power of thought and imagination, which is the initiating impulse for all creation. It brings this Divine power into full play, and contributes mightily to the strength and power of the emergence of a transfigured world.

Section V

Unfolding the Higher Plan

Chapter 17

Co-creating the Planetary Reservoir of Light

In the life of the world, and in the life of every incarnate soul, there comes a time when a decision and great choice is made which determines the future trajectory of the entity's evolutionary path. Such is the moment which now faces earth, humanity and all lives upon it.

The nature kingdoms have already made this choice and have raised their frequency to the incoming light and love, and are in a state of readiness to receive, absorb and radiate the next inflow of intensified light and love. The angelic world, too, is fully aligned with the choice to rise with the new energies, as the angels are already fully aligned with Divine will and always function within it.

The earth itself, as a living being (often called Gaia), has also made a full alignment with the higher plan as held by the Mother of the world, co-creating with the intention of the Divine Father/Creator.

The entire fulcrum of choice to shift the balance and initiate the Day of Revelation now lies with humanity. This process is nearly complete, and humanity is about to shift, so that more than 50% of people on earth will be oriented towards the light, and this will open the doors of revelation and allow a great inpouring of light and love.

Within these conditions and at this pivotal moment, it becomes extraordinarily important for every awakened soul and group to place their intention, conscious energy and support towards revealing and focusing on the light and love within all people, events and circumstances. It is of tremendous benefit to the plan to reinforce the light, in even its faintest flickerings, in every person and situation.

This increases the light present, draws it forth, and adds it to the gigantic collective pool of light present on earth being co-created by humanity and the higher spiritual powers. This makes it easier for others to be attracted to this collective light reservoir wherever it manifests, and bring its healing, calming and reassuring frequency into the hearts of those drawn into it.

It is this simple orientation towards the light, at first seen outwardly in others, and later discovered within oneself, which is tipping the balance towards the light rather than the dark, allowing the Day of Revelation to arrive.

Upholding the Light in Current Conditions

What does it mean to uphold the light in current world conditions? In each moment the duality of light and dark is present and playing itself out within the consciousness and conditions of human experience. Most people are confused by this and do not understand the nature of the choices being presented to them.

The dark is often grey, or concealed and masquerading as light, and deep discernment is required. What each conscious knower of the plan can contribute is a clear, insightful perception of the underlying reality and truth of what is present, and a formulation of clarifying statements about what is of the light and what is not.

Helping to illuminate for people what is true and lighted and what is not, spreads the light and assists people to choose to align with it, thus increasing the reservoir of light on the planet and within humanity.

Organizing and participating in group meditations amplifies the light, because it allows a greater intensity to be released into an energetic group field of multiple auras of people with different types of energies, focal points of consciousness, and levels of dissemination. Drawing people into these vortices of light also aligns them with higher frequencies of light, which stimulates each one's capacity to be light bearers.

It is important to understand this because many people do not yet fully understand the simple yet fundamental principles of working with energies and light. And an awareness of the percentage of humanity that is aligned with the light is important for the Day of Revelation.

The greater the percentage of humanity aligned with the light, the smoother and more complete will be the transformation. Beyond a certain time, the revelation will occur regardless of the human condition, but it is preferable to have the fullest possible human readiness and participation.

Criteria to Evaluate the Presence of Light

The following are some questions to help you know how to evaluate, at a given time, if some person, group or proposal is of the light or not. (Of course, people also change and light may be more or less present in various times and situations):

- How does this energy, situation, individual or group feel in your heart? Do you feel inspired and uplifted or lowered in your frequency?

- Does it embody or emphasize the unity of the One Life, or promote division and separation?
- How does this person, situation, or idea affect those people who are exposed to it – is loving, wise activity and co-creation encouraged and stimulated?
- Does the situation or idea recognize the creative power each individual has and encourage its full use for the good of all?
- Does it stimulate an awareness of the good of the whole or only a specific part of the whole?
- Is there any type of subtle coercion or manipulation, or does it respect the free will of each individual soul and seek to create conditions where this power can be most fully expressed in beneficial ways?

Ultimately, we need to open to the light, absorb it, and radiate it through our spiritual, mental, intuitive/emotional and etheric/physical bodies. This is the primary prerequisite for being able to perceive light, and encourage everyone to choose to live and move and have their being within the lighted dimensions.

Chapter 18

Current World Conditions

The conditions in the world have reached a near breaking point in the lives of millions of people, which creates greater impetus for the great shift. Conditions have been very difficult in the world for a long time, and it may appear to some people that there has been no spiritual help or intervention, which is not the case.

However, until now there has been no multi-dimensional, coordinated plan including the Galactics, so the primary approach was to send spiritual messengers to awaken humanity and indicate the way forward. Now, because of the needs of the solar system, and the decrees of the councils, decisive action on all levels is being taken, and continues to accelerate.

Understanding Energy Flows within Humanity

During this period in world history, there has been a growing withdrawal of consciousness from the negative aspects of three dimensional life in the world, and the search for an inner, abiding center of calm and security within each individual and like-minded groups. Although not all are directly engaged in this inner search, many people are discovering the futility of seeking peace, strength and love through outer accumulations or conditions.

Thus, a major part of the earth's population is preparing to receive all that the revelation of the plan will offer. Adjusting to the increased inflow of higher frequency energies to the earth, which can cause periods of over-stimulation or lethargy as our human bodies adapt, explains much about the current energetic dynamics within humanity.

Presenting the Principles of the Plan

At the same time, the awakened members of humanity are actively engaged in presenting the principles and programs which provide the foundations for the coming transfigured civilization.

All such statements and programs, made with a recognition of the One Life, are steadily anchoring the foundation stones for the great edifice of a liberated human civilization consciously co-creating with Spirit. All of humanity may not be able to fully visualize the beauty of the entire new civilization, but many people can see and respond positively to inspired innovations actually emerging today.

It is important to present these innovations and extrapolate them as harbingers of the coming new earth. Then the coming revelation will be seen as a natural outcome of what is already being built, and the reorganization of systems will be seen as the removal of obstacles to the full development of the new earth civilization. This is the essence of the current Light Alliance strategy and gives a plan of work for all active servers.

For example, interest in localized, organic agriculture being created amidst life in the cities is growing rapidly in the U.S. New laws are making more public land available for community gardens. Schools are creating gardens and greenhouses to teach children how to grow healthy food. Profitable, worker owned urban agriculture businesses are emerging in inner cities.

The Unstoppable Force for Higher Order Change

In order for a higher order change to occur, there needed to be a meeting of consciousness between an awakened portion of the human population and the higher Powers. Human thought needed to be oriented along the lines that the Light Alliance upholds.

There is now a meeting of the minds in the realm of how to improve human and planetary life. This synergy of thought with the Alliance, and a corresponding demand by humanity for help with real solutions, has rapidly coalesced in the past two years, and now has become an unstoppable force.

The recognition of the evils of our current economic system has crystallized in human recognition — the concentration of wealth and power, and the abuse of political systems by those with this wealth and power and their agents. The cry for reform, with mass demonstrations demanding change, as well as the intensity of the misery and suffering of great numbers of people, are all catalysts of the unfolding plan.

A study of world protests between January 2006 and July 2013 in 97 countries shows an increase from 59 protests in 2006, to 112 protests in only the first 6 months of 2013. Also, the size of protests has increased — 37 events had one million or more protesters, with some the largest in history — 100 million in India in 2013, and 17 million in Egypt in 2013. The main grievances are economic justice and austerity measures that are hurting many; the failure of political representation and political systems; and the rights of people.

Chapter 19

Higher Order Coordination of the Plan

Each individual who takes leadership by standing up for human rights, expressing legitimate grievances, or organizing mass movements is fulfilling their soul purpose. Every project with pure intention aimed at showing a better way forward for humanity is a soul guided endeavor.

On the level of soul consciousness, all such initiatives, when deeply resonant within dedicated individuals, are coordinated with the higher plan. This higher plan is part of the One Life and is transmitted to each living soul.

All these souls are working as an interrelated, powerfully irresistible movement of light, sweeping away the old forms by loving action guided by higher spiritual Powers. It is this flow of energy and awakening, stimulated by the vastly increased light, love and purpose being radiated to the planet, which is providing the necessary, widely-based anchoring of the plan by the Light Alliance. Without this response, the plan could not succeed.

Because of the decrees of the solar and galactic councils to free earth and humanity, lighted energies aligned with the plan are now available, and humanity is using them with great effect. And in a mutually reinforcing positive cycle, the more humanity accesses and uses these energies, the more energies can be released.

Thus it becomes extraordinarily important for each soul to ask themselves what they can offer, and how they can help in this great multidimensional movement to liberate the planet and all life. Turning within to contact your soul and asking for inspiration and guidance on how you can best help this great unfolding is the central spiritual focus of this time in human history.

We can make a useful comparison to the great struggle to liberate the planet during World War II, as the current times are the culminating effort to completely and permanently eliminate the dark forces from the planet. The battle now is on the subtle planes, and these times can call forth our greatest efforts to remain awake, immersed in the light and purpose of the Alliance, and upholding the light in all times and places.

Handling Human Resistance and Corruption

A question might arise about how the Light Alliance will deal with the negativity and resistance within humanity on the Day of Revelation. What will help will be a massive outpouring from higher spiritual sources of love and positive energy at an unprecedented level. (Some are calling this a "tsunami of love.")

This will raise the frequency of a majority of the people. This inflowing love and light all over the world, combined with the news of how the system is being reformed, will have a powerfully stimulating and reassuring effect on human consciousness.

In addition, the arrest of dark cabal leaders will allow people to see that their intuitive sense of the evil which was enveloping them was true. They will experience great subconscious relief when they see that this influence is being removed, and that new systems are being put in place which are transparent, fair and supportive of human well-being.

The issue of inequality in the world economic and social systems is now reaching a fever pitch of intensity, with rising demands for change. Economic inequality, injustice, greed, and levels of debt have never been higher, which has been a powerful stimulus to activate the mass consciousness to resist and demand a better life and true fairness.

This is part of the preparation for the Revelation, and humanity is fulfilling its rightful role in demanding change and fighting against the injustices and evils of the system. This intensifies the evocative call to action by the Light Alliance.

The Light Alliance (which includes many human members) will transform the corruption in most countries, where money given to help alleviate suffering is often stolen. Those corrupt people will be removed from power and others who are truly lighted will replace them.

There is a high level of corruption in people running the system in most major countries, and campaigns are underway to root out this corruption and remove those who are part of this system. And, once the standards of honesty, fairness and transparency are established, and the penalties for violation are clear, many people of integrity will be found who will gladly fill these positions.

The corrupted ones will be held accountable for their misdeeds and re-educated in places established for this purpose. They will hear people recount all the suffering they have caused them and will be given the opportunity to turn to the light. Those who refuse, will be taken off the planet into systems appropriate for their level of evolution, as a necessary corrective.

Believability and Managing Information

Once the process of revelation is underway, the greatest difficulty at first will be the believability factor. Humanity has been so manipulated, deceived and surrounded by false information that overcoming this rightfully warranted skepticism will be a top priority of the Light Alliance.

The Alliance has detailed plans of how to present this information to humanity as well as their intention behind the changes. Those who are conducting this operation will be identified as an international alliance of leaders who are taking steps to safeguard and help free humanity from the economic and political crisis around the world.

Some of the public leaders will be identified, and some of them already know they are part of a worldwide movement that is underway to remove the obstructing forces and change the system. However, they may not fully understand all the dimensions of the Light Alliance.

The cabal is already putting out fear-inducing disinformation about any changes being a takeover. However, the cabal's control of the media is being steadily undermined, and they are under threat of prosecution if they do not cooperate with the Alliance. This means there will be full reporting of the Day of Revelation.

The Reincarnation of High Souls

With the removal of the cabal, very high souls, including some of the geniuses of history, can reincarnate and come forward into public view in the world, which is part of the plan. The current period has been a cycle for courageous warriors, who came in to fight for freedom and defeat the cabal.

Once the cabal is removed, souls of great creative genius in all fields — politics, finance, science, social design, music, art and architecture — will come forward and help build the new transfigured civilization of light.

Combined with galactic systems and technologies, a world of glorious beauty, joy and creativity will be unfolded with the full understanding and conscious participation of all humanity, as well as the kingdoms of nature and the angels.

The appearance of many extraordinary children is already providing increasing evidence of soul abilities, and it soon will become self-evident that reincarnation is a fact. One recent public example is Amira Willighagen, the nine-year-old Dutch girl who sings opera like a much older great diva, and is clearly a reincarnated opera star.

The Role of the Galactics

Because the cabal has usurped powers and technologies which were meant as a gift to humanity, and because the cabal has been guided, until recently, by predators with evil intent, it simply was not possible for humanity to liberate itself without galactic assistance.

Although the Galactics have been uplifting the Earth since WWII, with the recent decrees to remove all dark forces from the earth, the Galactics are now allowed to directly support humanity to awaken from the illusion and free itself from the fear, oppression and darkness of the cabal. This process is accelerating very rapidly, leading to an apotheosis, when the truth about life on earth, its hidden history and the true story of humanity will be revealed.

Chapter 20

Working Out the Plan on Earth

Architecture and Gardens on the New Earth

New forms of architecture will be created with smooth, flowing, softer lines, in harmony with cosmic principles, which will uplift and inspire, rather than pull down, human consciousness.

Many old buildings in our cities will be removed with minimal disruption using galactic technologies, which will help eliminate pollution. In their place will be created buildings of great joy, light and beauty, which will literally sing to those who live within them, for they will be living beings, alive to the spirits of those inhabiting them.

These new buildings will be composed of a very similar type of energy to that used to create galactic ships. This new architecture will be seen in the early stages of transfiguration, and will be fully developed as it proceeds.

All manner and types of plants and herbs for food and healing will be grown, and weaving gardens throughout every city and all housing will be an essential part of the new architectural design.

The Cycles of Life in Nature

Just as there are cycles in the lives of civilizations, likewise there are cycles in the lives of nations, groups of all types, and in the lives of individuals. The nature kingdoms have cycles of waxing growth with strong livingness, and cycles of decline and decay.

In the world of appearances, it might seem that nature is in decline, but on the inner levels there is a building up of powerful life forces which are preparing to burst forth with unprecedented livingness and variety in the emerging cycle of revelation.

The Purpose of Current Weather Patterns

The drought, severe storms and extreme heat and frigid temperatures, causing so much unbalanced weather all over the world, are part of a process of purification of the earth. It may seem that with the drought in various regions, many trees will die and fires could be severe. But all these extreme conditions are forcing people to pay much closer attention to the condition of the planet and the interconnection of all life, and to realize that more care needs to be given to nature.

This will ultimately lead to a mass awakening to the relationship between consciousness and weather patterns, which is the purpose of the current situation. Although we have drought and frigid conditions, they will not be ultimately destructive of trees and wildlife, as it will be balanced out as the shift takes place.

When the shift occurs, temperatures will return to more normal ranges and the climate will stabilize. The Galactics will their use technologies to assist in this. The removal of the cabal and the raising of human consciousness will lift the earth's ecosystems into harmonic functioning with humanity and with higher solar and galactic patterns.

Scientists are also reporting that some extreme cold temperatures are having beneficial effects, as increased ice cover on rivers and lakes is protecting shorelines from erosion, and killing invasive insect species.

Examples of the Unfolding Plan

- *Fukushima Radiation* The question of whether the radiation from the Fukushima nuclear plant is being released into the skies and the Pacific Ocean and constitutes a danger to humanity is being widely discussed. However, this is being contained and neutralized by the Galactics, and the actual levels in the sea and air are not harmful, as has been verified based on careful, independent radiation monitoring.

- *The Keshe Foundation* (a group that has developed many free energy technologies) has stated it will help with the Fukushima radiation and implement other aspects of the plan using its new technologies. These are real and are part of the Light Alliance. The Foundation is aware of the Alliance and the Foundation's work assists all that is being done.

  The Foundation is being advised by Galactics who were the source of their discoveries. They were not stopped by the cabal because they have a superordinate degree of protection from the power of the devices they have created, as well as from the Galactics's assistance. They have an important role within the plan, which they are intent on fulfilling, and they will succeed.

- *Exoplanetary scientist Lisa Kaltennegger*, from Harvard University, is investigating 4,200 exoplanets orbiting distant stars, using computer models to determine which worlds could harbor life as we know it. She says the history of our planet's physical evolution could have been observed by extraterrestrials using spectral analysis, and they are looking at how this spectral fingerprint looks different for earth at different ages, to compare it to exoplanets they are studying.

- *UFO advocate named as new Obama advisor:* In early December 2013, former Clinton chief of staff John Podesta was named as President Obama's newest advisor. According to *The Huffington Post*, Podesta has more than once publicly urged the U.S. government to release any UFO files that could help scientists determine "the real nature of this phenomenon." At a news conference in 2002 at the National Press Club in Washington, D.C., Podesta called upon the U.S. government "to declassify [UFO] records that are more than 25 years old." On February 13, 2015, he tweeted that his biggest failure as chief of staff was not securing the disclosure of the government's UFO files.

Atomic Substance and
the Stages of Transfiguration

Chapter 21

The Transition from Molecular to Atomic Substance

The Absorption of Atomic Light

At this time, the focus of the Light Alliance is on the absorption of atomic light and love into all dimensions and bodies of individuals, families, groups, institutions and world systems. In order for light to be absorbed, there must be space within the molecular structure of these bodies to allow the entrance of atomic light substance.

This process of creating space within our bodies for new light is known as transmutation, changing a lower energy into a higher one.

Atomic substance is light, love and will from the three highest subplanes of the spiritual dimensions — the atmic (higher will), buddhic (intuitive love) and higher abstract mental planes of our multidimensional world.

Atomic substance is a lighter, finer, higher frequency energy which uplifts, inspires and frees people from the influence and control of lower energies. Depending on which higher subplane is accessed, it increases in potency as energies are sourced from the higher subplanes.

The Transition from Molecular to Atomic Substance

The molecules of substance in the physical/etheric, emotional and mental bodies of the unawakened individual are usually made up of atoms of the lower subplanes. This depends on the focus of his/her previous lives, and the degree to which spiritual aspiration to a pure and higher life has been present. The substance of the atoms of the lower subplanes are vibrating at a slower, heavier more grounded frequency.

Lower subplane energies make the physical/etheric body heavy, slow and lethargic; the emotional body prone to negative emotions such as fear and anger; and the mental body easily locked into rigid, predetermined modes of thought or with little original thought at all.

As you practice your spiritual intention for being more loving, harmless and giving, higher, fourth subplane substance is built into your bodies. The fourth subplane is the mediating plane between the three lower and three higher subplanes and is a doorway into the higher. It has the bridging function of opening a gateway into higher frequency and more lighted atomic substance. When atomic substance permeates the molecular atom's vibration, it raises it into the frequency of those lighter atomic vibrations. This happens as the atomic frequency gradually becomes the core energetic note of the substance of the bodies. This is often called "building the light body" in spiritual teachings.

This is the process carried out through transmutation, transformation and transfiguration, and is currently underway for earth and all lives upon it. When atomic substance begins to influence and ultimately becomes primary, all the great gifts so admired by humanity — charisma, radiance, artistic genius, inventive thought and universal compassion — become present, resulting in true lighted beings who contribute in powerful ways to the unfolding plan.

The subplanes are perceptible in a simple way by noticing the different atmospheres found in various locations such as bars, social settings, places of learning, houses of worship or spiritual power points in nature. Each of these is oriented to different subplanes by the consciousness that has been focused and expressed in these locations, both by human and subtle spiritual beings.

A similar process occurs within the environment of each human's physical, emotional and mental bodies, as one's consistent aspirations, thoughts, feelings and actions determine the quality of the substance attracted into and present in each body.

Thus, contact with and circulation of spiritual energies, including the energy of the higher will and the plan, draw in higher atmic substance.

Loving thoughts for the good of the world and the full expression of humanity's potential raise the quality of the substance in your mental body.

Universal compassion (based on a perception of the unity of all life) build in higher buddhic/intuitive substance into your emotional body.

Purification of your physical/etheric body with pure food, fresh air, sunshine and exercise allows higher subplane atomic substance to enter. Thus day-to-day decisions create the living laboratory for fully opening to and absorbing lighted atomic substance.

The Process of Opening to Atomic Substance

What allows light to be absorbed is the space created both within your consciousness and within your bodies, as this allows openings for its entrance. This requires a willingness and ability to transmute and release all lower frequencies which block the light's entrance.

Thus, it is necessary for each light worker to examine where these blockages might be found within his or her energetic systems, including the subconscious, and eliminate them as fully and rapidly as possible. This is done through inviting the love and light of higher dimensions into yourself, and absorbing it into your bodies as consciously as possible.

It also requires work to befriend, transform and integrate the subconscious dimension of your being so that you, the conscious self, become conscious of how it functions and can ask for its cooperation.

This entire process is simply the process of substituting a higher frequency energy and associated states of consciousness for a lower one. This brings about transmutation, transformation and ultimately transfiguration of your entire being.

Results of Integrating Atomic Substance

As atomic light enters, your physical/etheric, astral and mental bodies begin vibrating at these higher subplane frequencies. It is a steady and ongoing process of replacing denser molecular energy with lighter atomic substance, which is occurring within every individual, group and organization which has any openings whatsoever to such higher light.

When circulating through an individual's energetic system, atomic substance brings higher energy, endurance and freedom from the influence of the lower mass states of consciousness of fear, anxiety and separateness.

This transmuting and transforming light lifts your consciousness into an experience of the unity of life. This process is called by some people, "Moving from a carbon based energy form to one based on crystalline energy," which is another name for atomic light substance.

Chapter 22

What Are the Stages of Transfiguration?

The process of personal transfiguration begins at the moment an individual makes a free choice to consciously use their will, mind and heart to orient towards light and love in their life purpose and daily living. This choice by the conscious individual, however tenuous and flickering, is the beginning of the process of transmutation, transformation and ultimately, transfiguration.

Transmutation

Transmutation is the use of self-discipline, conscious choice and the invocation of soul light to clear away lower frequency patterns of thought, emotion and behaviors which do not reflect the innate Divine nature found deep within the heart of each incarnating soul. The desire to do so and to live at a higher level of service, oneness and joy results in the drive for transmutation.

This is often stimulated by a taste of these higher states of consciousness and being through spiritual experiences, which feed the aspiration to live in them more consistently. This is achieved when 25% of the molecular substance within one's physical, emotional and mental bodies is replaced with atomic light substance.

Transformation

As this process proceeds and accelerates, it attracts even greater attention from the soul, which radiates ever greater degrees of higher frequency atomic energy. This stimulates the revelation of other areas needing transmutation and brings to light many deep subconscious patterns, which can be resolved more rapidly by direct communication and cooperation with the subconscious.

Eventually the atomic light substance within the individual reaches 50%, and a transformation of the entire personality takes hold. Old habits fade out, and new feelings, thoughts and goals emerge. The soul then finds a greater opportunity to express its light, love and higher purpose through the conscious personality, and a life of radiatory service begins.

Transfiguration

As these higher frequency energies are more and more fully utilized, greater atomic light flows into the personality and all its vehicles, until the light of atomic substance reaches a high degree of presence, and replaces 75% of the molecular substance within the personality vehicles.

This means the light radiation of the Monad (the core center of our inner Divinity) can then begin to illuminate the soul/personality. This is known in the Ageless Wisdom as the third initiation or the transfiguration. Because of the unprecedented and intensified radiation of light now pouring into the planet and all life upon her, this transfiguration process is now underway for many lives on earth.

Many people are still in the stages of transmutation or transformation, all of which is supported and stimulated by this incoming light, love and power.

Those who have not oriented to light and love and entered the transmutation stage are finding it increasingly difficult to maintain their balance and current mode of living, and many will pass over during this process. This will contribute to the raising of the frequency of the earth, and is part of the plan for the transfiguration of the world.

The Transfiguration of the World

The same process of transmutation, transformation and transfiguration applies to the entire world and all of its structures. In many nations, the transmutation process arises as rebellion by various groups seeking to free themselves from oppressive control. Eventually, nations will align with their soul and higher purpose.

These processes will continue until the stage of transformation is reached. This will be facilitated with the launch of the Day of Revelation and the reform of their systems. This ultimately means that corrupt systems will be transformed, although it will take time for the effects of the Revelation to fully precipitate these changes.

Chapter 23

The Plan and the Current World Situation

The plan is an unfolding series of events, expressing energies from all dimensions that impact the earth. These include the galactic civilizations, the solar system, Shamballa, Hierarchy and the higher spiritual energies increasingly available. All these are causing the increasing refinement of the physical/etheric, astral and mental dimensions of our world.

The complexity of the interrelationships of these energies and forces is incomprehensible to ordinary, three-dimensional human understanding. All that is possible is a recognition of the effects of these energies on human beings, institutions, and the nature kingdoms.

All these energies in their sum total are stimulating the awakening of humanity, the activation of millions of efforts to improve human consciousness, and the conditions of life on earth.

The plan can be summarized as creating loving, lighted relationships within and between every life form on earth, as well as with lives on more subtle planes of being. Thus we can begin to comprehend the complexity of the plan.

The New Minimum Requirements to Be on Earth

The dark lodge has been completely opposed to the goals of the Divine plan for thousands of years, and with their removal and the dissipation of their power, the full expression of the plan now becomes possible.

This naturally moves consciousness and being into higher frequencies and creates new conditions and minimum requirements for being incarnated on earth. These include the acceptance of love as a fundamental principle of life, and an increasing capacity to embody and emanate love to all life.

It also includes light within the mind and heart, allowing for clear intuitive thought and recognition of truth versus falsehood. It is ascension out of fear, greed, and corrupted power into the world of loving relationships and contributions to the whole. These are the foundational principles of the new earth now emerging.

It is the joyful task of every light worker and every knower of the plan to absorb as much of this incoming atomic light and love as possible, circulating it to purify, transmute and transfigure our human personalities.

We then become a translucent vehicle for the higher light and love to radiate, inspire and uplift all within our circle of immediate contacts, and in the subtle levels of the world energetic fields, contributing to the transfiguration of the world.

World Situation Update

There has been tremendous progress on multiple levels, in both creating the necessary conditions and organizing the actions to accompany the release of energies to be precipitated as the Day of Revelation.

On the level of the Solar council, there is agreement that the coordination between all the groups and teams, both human, spiritual and galactic, has been highly developed, and that humanity's consciousness has continued to expand and awaken.

The practical plans for the new financial and political systems are fully developed, and thus the Day of Revelation can be initiated within the necessary time frame. This has been communicated from the Solar Council through Shamballa to the Masters.

The position of the dark lodge has continued to deteriorate as resources once controlled by them are slipping from their hands.

The military has undergone a major reorganization to remove those officers who were collaborating with the cabal. This process is now complete and the military is fully aligned with the Light Alliance and many officers know about the plan and are cooperating with it. This assures that the Day of Revelation will be fully supported by the military and their forces are available to assist, if this becomes necessary.

With every day that passes, humanity awakens more to how they have been manipulated and controlled, and people are seeing the dark forces more clearly for what they are. New actions are being taken by many institutions to reduce dealing with these dark forces wherever possible. Of course, there are still millions of people who are not awakened, because they are too drugged, confused or fearful to see clearly.

On the Day of Revelation, the spiritual energies of light and love will be greatly intensified, and many people will find it difficult to remain on earth. They will be relocated to places where they can continue their evolution on their own level. This will not happen all at once, but the intensified energy will allow people to naturally transition if they cannot adjust to the new energetic surroundings.

Weakening of the Cabal

Despite what we see on the news, the cabal's grip on the hidden, underlying power structures is weakening, which they realize. These systems are being closed down or removed from the cabal's hands day by day, and they know they are doomed, yet some continue to resist.

The Light Alliance awaits the signal from the higher Councils to launch the Day of Revelation, and continues to prepare for that day. Rather than the delay giving more time for the cabal to plan counterattacks — on the contrary — it allows them to weaken further.

Humanity, the Awakening Giant

Humanity, meanwhile, is steadily awakening to the true causes of the nature of the crisis it is in. It is a spiritual crisis — understanding how its own fear, greed and separation has allowed it to be controlled by the dark powers, and now awakening to the power and innate light and love within itself.

Humanity is realizing that it has given its power to these dark forces both within itself and in the systems it has accepted. Humanity is now in a process of taking back that power and its compliance and cooperation with these systems, and demanding a fair, equitable and compassionate world order.

This is the invocation of humanity, supported and upheld by the multidimensional light forces from the galactic civilizations, the spiritual councils and the planetary spiritual Masters.

This interdimensional power, now focused like a great laser light at the heart of the dark system, with its financial control of the world, will defeat the dragon of evil that has ruled the world for millennia. Despite all the cabal's efforts to terrify, confuse, distract and hide the truth from humanity, the true focal points of evil are being revealed, and light is being shown upon them, causing them to retreat.

Because of the strength of the backing from multiple dimensions of spiritual Powers, and the awakening of humanity, the complete defeat of the dark lodge is inevitable. Their time of ruling the planet is nearing its end, and the age of light is dawning.

Although the unfolding of the plan may seem slow, it is always done in right timing from the highest point of view. All that is being shared here will be eventually confirmed by events, which will be a great victory for humanity and the planet.

Chapter 24

Developments in the
Financial System and the World

Leaders of the dark cabal are being quietly arrested, indicted, or turned to the light. Many are also resigning in a steady stream. This is well known in the financial world, and is causing rapid deterioration of their power and morale.

The exposure by the International Consortium of Investigative Journalists (a key member of the Light Alliance) of billions of dollars hidden in secret offshore accounts had a worldwide ripple effect on the cabal, putting many of them on the defensive for illegal money laundering, avoiding taxes and other schemes. Governments around the world are passing laws to outlaw such practices, and some countries that have served as tax havens are now sharing information with tax and legal agencies all over the world.

There will be increasing pressure on the cabal leading to the Day of Revelation. It will be a culmination of the change to more lighted personnel in many institutions, and the announcement of the reorganization of banks and the political system.

Many agents of the cabal in the U.S. Congress will resign and some will not be re-elected. The money influence will be eliminated with the removal of people who are controlling the politicians. Not all will be arrested at once, because it has been decided it would be too threatening to the public, and could cause panic.

Corrupt banking leaders in J.P. Morgan, Goldman Sachs and Bank of America will have their turn to be indicted as the power of the Light Alliance grows and the cabal wanes. They are at the core of the control system, and when they fall, their grip will be completely broken.

There have been at least 70 suicides of bankers from HBSC, Deutsche Bank, J.P. Morgan and other banks in recent times. This is the result of their having to testify in investigations, and being threatened by the cabal if they tell the full truth. Since they cannot receive leniency from prosecutors for their cooperation, they would face long prison sentences. Some have chosen suicide rather than face these pressures, and others have been eliminated by the cabal.

Banks and Rechartering the Financial System

Many banks no longer have any sizable amount of gold as real assets because behind the scenes, the Light Alliance is gaining control of the world's gold. This fact will be kept hidden, so there will not be a panic about gold that could destabilize the system. Thus, closing the current banks will have less impact because they do not control actual assets like gold.

Once illegitimate mortgage debt is annulled, the banks will no longer control homes through mortgages. Banks will become empty shells, and then can be easily re-chartered on an entirely new basis as public service entities. They will then actually serve economic activity without stealing through charging interest on all money, which has created huge debt for ordinary people.

U.S. and UK Regulators Investigating
Banks Manipulating Foreign Exchanges

- *New York banking regulator Benjamin Lawsky* is seeking documents from some of the biggest banks in foreign exchange trading, including Deutsche Bank, Goldman Sachs and Barclays, according to reports, as a global probe into possible market manipulation widens, the UK Telegraph reported.
- *The U.S. Justice Department is pushing Wall St banks to plead guilty to criminal charges that they manipulated the prices of foreign currencies* in the $5.3 trillion-a-day currency markets.
- *Martin Wheatley, chief executive of Britain's Financial Conduct Authority*, said recently that his watchdog group's probe could extend into 2015, and that the allegations it is looking into are "every bit as bad" as the Libor manipulation scandal.
- *More than 20 traders* across Wall Street have either been put on leave, suspended or fired since the foreign exchange investigations were formally announced.

Statements of Key Financial Leaders

- *Janet Yellen*, the new chairwoman of the U.S. Federal Reserve, is aligned with the values of the Light Alliance, but is not fully aware yet of the plan and what is unfolding. She will be informed, and will align with it. Her recent statements indicate she is very concerned about unemployment and its impact on families.
- *Christine Lagarde*, Director of the IMF, is aware of some aspects of the plan for financial reform and is cooperating with the Light Alliance. In

a recent speech in London, Lagarde said, "We need a financial system for the 21st century...where the global good prevails...With financial oversight that is effective in clamping down on excess, while making sure credit gets to where it is most needed. We need a new 21st century multilateralism to get to grips with big-ticket items like climate change and inequality. On these issues, no country can stand alone."

• *Jim Kim*, President of the World Bank, is moving the bank in the right direction. He is aware of the plan for financial reform in a general outline, but not the details. He recently told Arianna Huffington, "Many people can benefit from meditation." He also said he was pleased to hear that the World Economic Forum had made income inequality one of its priorities this year. He also pointed out the Oxfam report that concluded that the top 85 people in the world control as much wealth as the bottom half of the population. "That's as stark as it gets," he said.

• *Ban Ki Moon*, Secretary-General of the UN, was under the influence of the cabal, but is now mostly aligned with the Light Alliance, and he knows the plan to a large degree.

Other Developments

• *Genetically modified organisms (GMOs)*, will be phased out in the new civilization. They have not severely damaged humanity's health, but if continued over an extended period, they would. The Galactics are working to neutralize their effects on humanity, but not their effect on lab rats, so their harmful effects can be evident to all.

• *An alternative to GMOs* is radiowave treated water, a groundbreaking new Irish technology, which energizes water and massively increases the output of vegetables and fruits by up to 30%. The plants are not only bigger, but largely disease-resistant, meaning huge savings in expensive fertilizers and harmful pesticides. Extensively tested in Ireland and several other countries, the inexpensive water treatment technology is now being rolled out across the world. The technology makes GMOs obsolete and also addresses global warming by simply converting excess CO_2 into edible plant mass.

• *In religion, true peace* is beginning to emanate into the world field except for the most fanatical, who are steadily being isolated within their cultures. Many interfaith initiatives are growing everywhere. For example, the government of President Hassan Rouhani of Iran has donated $400,000 to Tehran's only Jewish hospital. Rouhani's brother, who made the donation, said, "Our government intends to unite all ethnic groups and religions, so we decided to assist you."

- *The United Religions Initiative* is working in many different countries with over 600 Cooperation Circles, each with at least three members of different religions. They are cooperating to heal the wounds of conflicts, develop economic and social justice, support the environment, and create authentic dialogue among people of different faiths. They are helping create a world where compassion, understanding and cooperation are the guiding principles.
- *Fossil fuel divestment* is growing, as 17 foundations controlling nearly $1.8 billion in investments have united and are pulling their money out of companies that do business in fossil fuels. In addition, 22 cities, 20 religious organizations, nine colleges, and six other major institutions have signed up to divest themselves of investments in the top 200 coal, oil and gas producing companies identified by the Carbon Tracker Initiative, based in London. Freeing up these resources allows these organizations to invest in the renewable energy sector, and they are finding that this move makes economic sense and provides higher returns.

Political Changes:

- *A Zone of Peace* was declared by the 33-nation Community of Latin American and Caribbean States (CELAC), who signed a declaration promising not to intervene in other countries' internal affairs and to resolve disputes peacefully. Leaders recognized "the inalienable right of every state to choose its political, economic, social and cultural system."

  They also put in writing the need to resolve differences "through dialogue and negotiation or other forms of peaceful settlement established in international law." The declaration also reiterated the need for total, global, nuclear disarmament and highlighted the ongoing importance of the 1967 Tlatelolco Treaty, which established the region as a nuclear-free zone.

Meditation on Atomic Light Substance

Begin by breathing in peace and stillness, and focus on each of the three higher subplanes (the atmic or will dimension, the buddhic or higher intuition, and the higher mind).

Visualize atomic light coming into each of these three subplanes. Allow your soul to transmit the degree of atomic substance that is appropriate for you into your mental, emotional and physical/etheric bodies.

Allow this higher frequency light energy to circulate throughout your bodies, bringing greater peace, strength and inspiration into your being.

See this light flowing all the way down through each of your chakras or energy centers, and out your feet, connecting you with the earth and with the Divine Mother.

See the energy of the Mother rise back up through your feet and legs, see it rising up into your heart, blending with the atomic light coming from your soul above.

Section VII

The Organization of
the New Civilization

Chapter 25

Light Groups and the Matrix of Love

The core organizing principle for the new civilization is based on the synergies of consciousness which occur in group and intergroup co-creation. The possibilities of group creation are just beginning to be realized by humanity, and a multitude of experiences, experiments and expressions of group activities are underway. Many of these are well intentioned, and many have mixed motivations and therefore mixed results.

The principles and methods of all light groups, whether consciously associated with the great multidimensional Alliance of Light or not, are based on the matrix of love as the core organizing principle. This means that light groups hold each of their members, their group purpose and the well-being of the world with love, aligned with the higher purposes of the plan (whether consciously realized or not).

This matrix of love becomes an operating field within which all plans, group thought and activities are implemented. This is the definition of a true light group. An important part of this process is bringing each member into resonance with love and into alignment with the group's higher purpose. This requires the processes of transmutation, transformation, and ultimately transfiguration, as we have previously discussed.

A core teaching which will be given during the period leading up to and after the Day of Revelation is about how to create and develop joyful, productive and aligned group work. At their highest level of functioning, groups are meant to be stations for receiving, transducing and transmitting energy within the body of humanity.

What is most needed is humanity's clear understanding of the role of purpose and plan, so the sense of meaninglessness, helplessness and futility is overcome. All this will be replaced with a clear vision of humanity's place and function within the higher plan, and how that can be actualized on earth.

This can be most effectively transmitted by groups with a diverse membership, focused on different levels of consciousness, and thus reaching many levels within humanity. Such groups can be created by all who receive and understand the significance of the unfolding plan for the transfiguration of the world.

Principles of Light Groups

The formation of groups into ordered patterns representing human diversity is a core aspect of the plan. The principles for new groups are not rigid, but rather are guiding practices that will represent key functions required for a healthy civilization:

1. The internalization of an unalterable ethic of stewardship, of both humanity and the nature kingdoms.
2. An emphasis on healing, regenerating and reorganizing all aspects of life to ensure the well-being of all living creatures.
3. A recognition that all voices need to be heard and understood, while acknowledging that the voices of those with the greatest vision, compassion and understanding of right timing need to be most carefully listened to.
4. The encouragement of a steady inflow of creative, new ideas and inventions that serve and uplift the whole.
5. The creation of an order and stability which provides the basic necessities and security to all members of human societies and the natural world.
6. A predictability and established organization focused around cycles and rhythms, of both the natural world and planetary, solar and cosmic cycles.
7. An awareness that group leadership will be based on soul maturity and wisdom with the responsibility of group members to listen intuitively for the source of greatest wisdom and compassion, and the highest good of all, regardless of from whom it is emerging.
8. An understanding that the principle of synthesis is the keynote of the new world, and the highest path is found in a synthesis of the most clear-sighted, loving and practical plans of any group.

The understanding and living of these principles will be the foundations of the new earth, which will be incorporated into every level of society, from individuals to families, communities, business and political organizations, nations, and the planet as a whole. This will steadily grow into full flowering as the new higher frequency conditions of consciousness are absorbed by humanity and expressed by all nations and cultures.

A core capacity which will be shared with all who choose is the capacity to quiet the many dimensions of your being and become open to inspiration and guidance from those who are offering higher wisdom to humanity.

These wisdom sources can include your own soul, as well as groups such as ashrams on the inner planes where Masters and high initiates work together for uplifting and guiding humanity. Understanding how to evaluate information and energies received in this way, and how to avoid distortions and misuse of them, will be a core teaching in the new civilization.

Chapter 26

The Organization and Limitations of Dark Groups

Since certain groups today are being used by the dark lodge, it is important to understand the differential factors between those using the principle of group energy for evil purposes and those using it for the light. Dark groups, by definition, are incapable of deep trust and love, which is the energy which harmonizes, uplifts and creates group coherency and power. Such dark groups do not respect human free will and are always trying to manipulate or control their members.

Because members of dark groups never can fully trust each other, and because their purposes are in opposition to the plan, their access to higher dimensional energies is always limited.

And because they work with the dark, low-frequency energies which are anti-evolutionary, those who participate in such groups are inevitably weakened, and often destroyed by the energies present within these groups. This dynamic guarantees that the dark side will always be overcome by the light powers, within a greater cycle of time.

It is upon these truths that knowers of the plan take their stand, with a recognition of the ultimate invincibility and victory of light over darkness and evil in any system.

The Organization of Dark Groups

The organization of dark groups is control by instilling fear, separation, and competition for scarce life resources, with the resulting conflicts and wars. All of this is done with great cunning and careful structuring. The founders of the dark lodge from outside the planet were well-versed in such techniques, and had the advantage of previous experience in exploiting planetary populations and resources, as well as having more advanced technologies and psychic capabilities.

This allowed them to build control systems using both outer structures, such as interlocking directors of companies and organizations, but also psychotronic veiling of consciousness, stimulation of fear and blocking access to humanity's true inner light.

Because these systems can only be effective if kept concealed, one of the most potent developments within the unfolding plan is the unveiling of these webs of control. This allows humanity, even at this early stage of revelation, to see how the system has been manipulated for centuries. The types of groups which the dark lodge has created and used thrive only in secrecy. They use lies, false front organizations, and disinformation to keep humanity from discovering their existence and true purpose.

As the revelations of the secret purposes and functions of this web of manipulation is revealed, the structure of the dark groups is being shaken to its core, and now is in disintegration. This is causing them to try and change their apparent purposes to more seemingly benign ones, like resolving the wealth inequality in the world. Recent statements about concern for economic inequality at the World Economic Summit at Davos are examples of this.

The methods of dark groups include false propaganda through the controlled media, creating fear-generating thoughtforms, false flag operations such as 9/11 and other incidents. They control their group members through intimidation and threats, using murder and fake suicides of any who would reveal their operations.

Their methods are the antithesis of the principles and methods of light groups, especially honoring human free will is a sacred principle.

It is important to make the distinction between the two groups very clear, so there can be no confusion in people's minds about the difference.

Current Status of the Struggle with the Cabal

The struggle on the front lines for breaking the power of the cabal is very intense on the inner levels. The cabal is desperately trying every ruse and trick possible to obtain more money and maintain themselves in power, but all is in vain. They are killing bankers, and using fake suicides to destroy those people who would reveal their activities. They also had a plan to secretly murder a large number of other bankers to protect themselves, but this was prevented, as steps have been taken to end this activity.

One of the Asian groups of the Light Alliance is offering protection to those in danger if they will tell what they know. There will be prosecutions as part of the process, but pardon and forgiveness will be offered to those who committed lesser crimes and repent. The dark leaders will be given this opportunity, but without a sincere change of heart, they will be removed from the planet.

There will be an adjustment in the value and use of gold, but all that has been earned legitimately will be safe for its owners. The assets which banks have confiscated through the manipulation of the financial system will be taken and made available for the good of all.

Because of the complexity of the system, the initial changes to banks and currencies will be relatively rapid, but the full integration of the plan to confiscate illegitimate wealth and distribute it to the people will extend over some time. The spiritual forces are totally confident that this plan will be put into place without being subverted in any way.

Chapter 27

The Light Alliance Group Network

The Light Alliance, both on earth and in its higher ashramic and galactic dimensions, is a network of groups at many different levels of consciousness, understanding and capacities. Some are nearly entirely focused on the practical details of engineering the needed monumental shifts in the financial system, which are extraordinarily complex. Other groups are organizing the collection of evidence and planning the judicial proceedings against the cabal.

Other groups are planning actions to be taken on the Day of Revelation to take control of major financial and political systems and remove all cabal members from power. These are primarily groups of humans, who have been given enough understanding of the plan by sources they trust, that they are willing to take the steps necessary to support its unfolding. They are at very little risk, as they are protected by each other and the spiritual power of the Galactic Light Alliance.

The next level are those groups with a larger vision of all the groups implementing the plan and creating the new civilization, and how all these aspects function together. These are members of the Ashram of Synthesis or those under its guidance, who are helping to coordinate all the many group activities and energies into one worldwide movement of light, with millions of individuals and groups working together.

This coordination is organized within the Ashram of Synthesis, with many different focalizing centers, which are councils of evolved spiritual individuals (known as initiates) who oversee and guide all the vast numbers of groups from the inner, spiritual dimensions. Within the outer working groups are individuals who either have direct conscious contact with a member of the Ashram, or are able to be impressed with the guidance they need to move the group forward in coordination with the great plan. The members of the Ashram with this function are known as the "bridges" who maintain contact and communication with all the practical teams.

At another level within the Ashram are those members who are in contact with the higher councils such as Shamballa, and a very few who have contact with the Solar council. Most direction for the Ashram comes from Shamballa and occasionally from the Solar council.

Shamballa provides information on the unfolding status of the plan and where energies need to be applied for what purpose. It provides information on the activities of the galactic forces, expected developments and their timing, and the status of the dark lodge's disintegration.

There is nothing hidden from the Galactic Light Alliance about the dark lodge's intentions, plans, activities and secrets. This is due to the spiritual powers of the ashram as well as galactic technologies, and coordination of efforts and information from all levels so nothing can be hidden. The Galactics have monitoring capacities far beyond anything we know, and information is shared with all who need it to implement the Plan.

Planning for the Galactics' full disclosure to humanity is being developed among all the councils, coordinated through the Ashram, which is receiving information and guidance from these higher levels. Representatives from Sirius are present on the Shamballa council, along with Pleiadians and Andromedans. Other civilizations also offer input and support, so the comprehensive overview is vast.

What happens on earth affects the whole galaxy through the Law of Progression. All will rise to a higher level with the liberation of the earth, and the frequency of the entire system will be lifted into greater light and joy. It is rare for a planetary population to go through the transfiguration while people remain in their bodies. This has happened in a few places but it is very unusual.

Groups Attuning to Nature

With the raising of the frequency of the earth after the Day of Revelation, the nature of group work and experience will also undergo a shift. Groups working together to raise consciousness and create a unified field within higher dimensions will find their perception enhanced and their capacities multiplied. Such groups will be able to enter more fully into the consciousness of the mineral, plant and animal kingdoms, and know what these kingdoms are experiencing and what they need.

These groups will also perceive the energetic web linking all the nature kingdoms together with the human world, and understand exactly how human thought and emotion affects these kingdoms by seeing their energetic impacts. This type of perception will eventually spread from groups into the prevailing consciousness of humanity, resulting in a complete change in human thought, emotion and activities in relationship to nature.

The perception of the world of nature spirits, devas and angels will also be open to such groups and steadily be integrated into human awareness. Those individuals and groups who already have such capacities are precursors of the state of consciousness which will be widespread within humanity in the new earth.

This will be possible because the matrix of love will be greatly magnified by the energies released on the Day of Revelation. It is upon this type of perception and awakening of consciousness that a completely new relationship with the natural world will be established, which is one of the core foundations of the new civilization.

Groups Co-creating with Galactics

Other groups will come together with the purpose of communicating with and assisting in the preparations for the galactic civilizations to make their presence known to humanity. This will occur sometime after the Day of Revelation, so co-creative work to prepare humanity for this event will be needed and is an essential part of the Transfiguration Plan.

With the shift in energy and consciousness on the earth and the full removal of the cabal from positions of power, the entire atmosphere within humanity and on earth will greatly improve. Once people fully understand and experience that they will have all they need to live well, including food, shelter, clothing, healthcare, education and creative opportunities, a field of great joy and relaxation will spread over the world.

Subconscious survival fears will steadily dissipate and trust in the benevolence of life and the universe will grow. This will be due to the process of the planet moving out of its long period of darkness and into the light of planetary liberation. All will have the freedom to live, laugh, create and expand as far as each can imagine. It will be a renaissance of the liberated human spirit, the likes of which has never been seen before on earth.

Groups focused on communication with galactic civilizations will have specific tasks to undertake to educate humanity about how they have been conditioned to fear and reject galactic contact. This was because the cabal knew the Galactics were the greatest threat to their power. This will also explain the attempted suppression of information about contact with their space ships and even direct meetings with Galactics by many individuals.

Evidence of what humanity has seen and experienced throughout history as contact with these civilizations will be presented, as a means to prepare human consciousness for actual full contact. This contact will occur when it is determined that humanity is sufficiently prepared, with an accurate understanding of what galactic civilizations really are, and their benevolent intentions. The plan includes ultimately giving an opportunity for earth to join the Galactic Light Alliance if humanity so chooses.

Healing Groups

There will be other groups who will focus on healing earth's ecosystems, reweaving the etheric web where needed, and working in close co-creation with the angels and devas of entire regions. These groups will be guided in their work by members of the Ashram, some of whom will be incarnated on earth, and others who will be assisting from the inner planes.

As a result of the Day of Revelation and succeeding events and expansions of consciousness, the veils between the dimensions will be steadily reduced and ultimately eliminated. This means that the fourth and fifth kingdoms, the conscious world of humanity and the world of spiritual Masters and guides, will be in accessible and natural contact.

Co-creation, combining inspiration, vision and insights from these dimensions, as well as from the nature kingdoms and the galactic civilizations, will be the new fields of dynamic exploration. These will allow the rapid creation of new forms of energy, food, housing, transportation, and recreation, which will be multidimensional, as well as beautiful and beneficial to all life on earth.

Chapter 28

Focus of Groups in the New Earth

The focus of groups in the new earth will shift from primarily creating activities to collectively raising their consciousness into higher dimensions. They will perceive what is present in these dimensions, receive energies, and then direct these lighted energies for the benefit of the new world.

Plans and visions of how the new Divine order can be built will be present on the higher planes, and these will be received by many groups. The similarity of impressions will be an indicator that these are coming from a higher source. Social and cultural details will be added by each group, but there will be common principles and outlines of how to build a new society.

Many exchanges will emerge between groups around plans for human betterment that they have inwardly received. This will be an expansion of what is already occurring between groups, but at a much higher level of inner congruence and synthesis. It will be a joyful experience to see the outlines of the new civilization emerging in different countries and cultures, all inwardly guided and linked with the same source.

There will be opportunities for everyone to participate, from village farmers working together to improve their crops and their capacity to feed their people nourishing food, to inventors working together to create new technologies that serve human life. These opportunities will release people from drudgery into the freedom of self-development and self-expression of their gifts in fields such as music, poetry, art and other creative individual and group activities.

World leaders will be meeting together in a regular rhythm, to help each country solve their problems and improve the lives of their people. A new international ethic will unfold, based on the inner experience of the oneness of all life.

All this interaction and interrelationship on inner and outer levels will lead to an increasing telepathic rapport within humanity. This will be stimulated by the energetic shifts on the planet that are bringing a great inflow of love and unity, and enhanced mental capacity for all humanity. The removal of the veils over the consciousness of humanity will greatly accelerate all these transformations, and there will be a reduction in subconscious survival fear through programs for human well-being.

No aspect of human life will be unchanged, from financial and political life to religious understanding, human relationships, and openness to the natural and angelic worlds, as well as the energy used to power the entire civilization. Such complete change is inconceivable to most people under the current conditions, but with the Day of Revelation, the changes will begin and a new life for all humanity will emerge.

Meditative Exercise on Groups in the New Civilization

Consider groups you are currently part of and reflect on what you would do differently when the veils are removed and all are functioning in a higher dimensional frequency. Meditate on how these groups can be brought into deeper alignment with these higher principles and practices, and into greater rapport and connection with other groups:

1. The internalization of an unalterable ethic of stewardship, of both humanity and the nature kingdoms.
2. An emphasis on healing, regenerating and reorganizing all aspects of life to ensure the well-being of all living creatures.
3. A recognition that all voices need to be heard and understood, while acknowledging that the voices of those with the greatest vision, compassion and understanding of right timing need to be most carefully listened to.
4. The encouragement of a steady inflow of creative, new ideas and inventions that serve and uplift the whole.
5. The creation of an order and stability which provides the basic necessities and security to all members of human societies and the natural world.
6. A predictability and established organization focused around cycles and rhythms, of both the natural world and planetary, solar and cosmic cycles.
7. An awareness that group leadership will be based on soul maturity and wisdom with the responsibility of group members to listen intuitively for the source of greatest wisdom and compassion, and the highest good of all, regardless of from whom it is emerging.
8. An understanding that the principle of synthesis is the keynote of the new world, and the highest path is found in a synthesis of the most clear-sighted, loving and practical plans of any group.

Freeing Media Channels and Earth's Auric Sphere

Chapter 29

Freeing and Opening the Media to Light

The Needs of Humanity Today

One of the greatest needs people have is for clarity, understanding and confidence that the world is moving in a positive direction with higher guidance and support. So many people are lost in fear and speculation, with no real anchor points for a realistic optimism about the world. This leads to insecurity, separative behaviors, and loss of courage and energy. But each of us can provide the vision and understanding that people are seeking. We can offer proof from what is happening, and also from what has not happened — the fearsome predictions that have not come true.

We can also ask people to look within their hearts and ask themselves whether they really intuit the world will continue as it is or be destroyed — or will it come through this crisis successfully? Their response, of course, will depend upon their personal psychological mindset, and people have been so controlled and manipulated that they often hardly know who they are. That is why it is so important to work towards freeing humanity. People are waking up, and seeking answers, a higher vision and ways to move into a clearer, higher life.

The Current Status of the Unfolding Plan

The conditions in the world are such that many people are anticipating a powerful release of energies which will extend throughout all dimensions and touch the heart of the earth itself. This inflow will anchor light, love and spiritual will in the earth and in the minds and hearts of humanity in ways never before seen or experienced.

The central work now is to prepare human minds and hearts to receive and work with these inflowing energies to the maximum degree possible. All meditations invoking, transmitting and anchoring light and love into the planes of manifestation on earth are absolutely essential to the unfolding plan.

From the base which has been established within the planetary network of light, an even greater radiance is steadily permeating the substance of earth and the dimensions of human living. This facilitates the work of all those who are offsetting the strategies of the cabal, and helping cabal members fully realize that they are now defeated, and their best course is to surrender.

Opening the Media to Light

Throughout history, there have been many attempts by the forces of light to redirect humanity's consciousness onto the higher pathways. Many devices have been used, including stories and myths, such as the ancient Greek and Roman gods and goddesses, King Arthur and the Knights of the Round Table, and many others. Music has also been a vehicle, with ballads and stories to give guidance towards a higher way of life.

Plays and dramas, from Greek tragedies to Shakespeare to modern movies and television (such as Star Trek) have also been used. All of these have helped to incrementally raise human awareness and understanding of the true principles of spiritual life and how to live a fulfilled and joyful life.

In today's world, with all the tools of communication now available, the opportunities have never been greater to reach and lift humanity. Yet much of the media is occupied with programs which transmit the cabal's message that darkness is overwhelmingly powerful, that there is much to fear, and that violence, greed and selfishness are innate in human nature. Current events are usually presented in ways that serve the purposes of the cabal for control, intimidation through fear, inciting hatred and violence and endless threats to humanity's survival. This keeps people on edge so they can be more easily manipulated and controlled.

This misuse of existing communication channels is steadily being brought to an end through exposure and prosecution of wrongdoing by media barons. The uprising of new channels of information at many levels, and the emergence of courageous individuals who are exposing corruption and evil-doing at great personal risk, are opening up opportunities for a revolution in the use of these media channels.

It is an essential and significant aspect of the unfolding plan that media channels become outlets for the light of truth that humanity is longing for. We can each focus our energy on these channels of communication, seeing them becoming unblocked and opening up to truth, to new visions of the spiritual potential of human beings, and to the nature of humanity's relationship to one another, the natural world and the cosmos.

This process is already underway, and can be greatly accelerated by visualizing the world communication system becoming filled with light and higher purpose, and control moving from the cabal into the hands of the Light Alliance.

This inner work will greatly facilitate the plan, as there is an important need for the truths about humanity's existence and the truth about events now occurring to be more fully and openly presented. This will help prepare humanity for the shifts that are coming, and allow the transformation of financial and political systems to be brought about with minimal fear and resistance.

Chapter 30

The End of the Cabal

There comes a time in any campaign when the tide turns, and the light energies marshaled by the prevailing powers begin to overwhelm the dark opposition. They lose heart, realizing they are facing defeat. They then consider their options: they can fight on, knowing they will be destroyed; they can surrender and cooperate; they can try to flee and hide away in prepared locations; or they can choose to end their own lives.

All of these choices are now being exercised by members of the cabal. None of these choices are serving them except surrender and cooperation. Those who continue to fight will be defeated; those who run away will be found; and those who end their lives will still be responsible for all their actions and have to balance their negative karma in future lives. Such is the nature of cosmic justice.

Forgiveness will be offered by the Light Alliance, but it must be earned by the offenders through true repentance. All those who turn to the light and join the Light Alliance will be re-embraced. All will be held accountable and handled with merciful justice.

It is important at this stage of the campaign that all light forces maintain the pressure on the opposition until complete victory is won. This includes all meditation work, positive thought and visioning for the future, development of new projects, circulation of information about the plan and its current status, continued exposure of the dark activities and plans of the cabal, and building rivers of light between all positively oriented groups worldwide.

This is an exceedingly challenging time on earth, with a great point of tension being held by the Light Alliance. The energies will only increase in intensity during the current period.

Each of us has a role to play in our appointed place, and it is up to each of us to carry it out as clearly and beautifully as possible. With all partners in Light Alliance continuing their pressure on the dark lodge, we will be successful. Let us all dedicate every effort to this noble cosmic purpose.

The Surrender of the Cabal in the Banking Sector

There has been a crucial victory in the battle with the dark Lodge, as a major portion of the cabal has surrendered. This is in the banking sector, and includes more than half of the banks, including the Vatican bank, which have agreed to turn over their financial control to the Light Alliance, which is now evident in the complete reorganization of the bank being directed by Pope Francis. Also, the proliferation of investigations is part of the pressure being put on the cabal and their position is substantially weaker.

The remainder are being helped to realize they cannot maintain their power and wealth, and it will be beneficial for them to cooperate and join the victorious side. Those who refuse will be made powerless and unable to influence outcomes. They will be contained within energetic spheres if necessary.

A large percentage have surrendered, which is a major shift in the power dynamics of the world, yet many remain unchanged. This is the axis of transformation — to convince those remaining that their best choice is to surrender their power and wealth voluntarily.

Only those who are most obdurate and resist all cooperation will be arrested. There will be some arrests, but not on a mass scale. This is a change in the plan, which is always evolving based on shifts in consciousness and conditions. This is now seen as the best path forward. It will create less disruption and radical change, and provoke less reaction within humanity.

It is important not to mistake efforts towards a negotiated shift for weakness, as the power is now in the hands of the Light Alliance. The Alliance simply chooses to use it in a different way. A high percentage of the cabal will ultimately agree to surrender, and most of their illicit wealth will be taken. It is difficult to see this loss of power in the mainstream media because it is still controlled by the cabal.

There are major movements going on within the financial system to indict many of the key cabal members. This is how the Light Alliance is pressuring them to surrender — by giving them no options for escape. The enforcement has been strengthened by members of the Light Alliance moving into regulatory agencies.

Iceland's method of indicting corrupt banking leaders, and completely reorganizing the financial system, was an example of how the world system can be reformed. This will be used as a model so that the shift will appear as an evolution in response to the crisis, rather than a revolution and overthrow of the entire system. This is why there will not need to be mass arrests, except of the most resistant.

Each day that passes sees the cabal weakening, losing members, and fighting among themselves, while the Light Alliance is growing in influence and control. Large numbers of Light Alliance members are spread throughout system in every field, and their radiation, combined with the inflowing spiritual energies, is steadily transforming the system.

Those whistleblowers who have questioned and objected to what was being done by the cabal are being given strength, reinforcement and courage to stand against it, to speak out and press for change from within the system. This is occurring in government, corporations, and educational and religious institutions. Healthcare (especially in the U.S.) is one of the last holdouts, but this too will go through significant change relatively soon.

Chapter 31

The Expansion of the Earth's Auric Sphere

The Evolution of Light Circulation

We are approaching a time which is unlike any period in the history of the earth. Never before has there been such a close knit, lighted web of energies circulating, with a constant flow of communication and exchanges between individuals, groups and nations.

On the inner planes there is a corresponding increase in the flow of energies throughout the planetary grids of light on the etheric, emotional and mental levels, which is aiding in regenerating the health of the earth. As is well known, when energy fully circulates through all centers and dimensions of any being's life, greater health and well-being results.

The huge number of meditations, visualizations, prayers and positive thoughts by all types of individuals and groups of every spiritual tradition worldwide is accelerating the circulation throughout the network of light. This network was previously built and connected from center to center, power point to power point, by lines of light.

Now what is occurring is that these lines or strands are expanding into ever widening bands or streams of light flowing between all types of awakened centers — individuals, groups and countries. As lines of connection become streams and then vast rivers of light and love flowing between and among groups, the light in the world evolves from being a network, to an auric field, to a reservoir or pool of light, into a complete field of light. The entire Earth is thus infused and surrounded within a sphere of light.

With the ever increasing inflow of light from the center of the galaxy, and from galactic civilizations, Shamballa and the spiritual Hierarchy, the light is finding many new anchoring and radiatory points within individuals and groups. Also, the intensity of the spiritual energy flowing through those already receptive is being magnified, increasing the anchoring of the light within their bodies and surroundings.

There is a corresponding fuller embodiment and radiation of light within the nature kingdoms, which is greatly increasing the light within the earth. The atomic substance has anchored more completely, making the conditions for the cabal more and more difficult.

But there are still places on earth with concentrations of darkness like some countries in the Middle East and Africa. Even though ancient karmic patterns are being worked out, these too, are being influenced by the light. Hatred, violence and war are being burned out through their extreme expression. The situation in Syria is nearly completed karmically, and a resolution will be developed with higher spiritual help.

Eventually exhaustion sets in, and the desire for peace arises. This is being supported by the inflow of strengthening light and love, and these energies will ultimately become the unified frequency of humanity. The Israeli-Palestinian conflict is one of the most intractable of all, but it, too, will be resolved when the timing is right.

What We Can Do

There is a real and profound need for all those who embody the light to any degree to clarify the way forward into greater light to those who are seeking positive change. This means helping people understand how to release all that is holding them captive in lower frequencies, and how to align with reliable sources of lighted vision and universal love.

For most, this is helping them make a connection and ongoing alignment with their soul, so they establish a center of clarity and purpose within themselves. The body of lighted people around the world is expanding every day.

The field of love and light can be greatly reinforced by meditations to bring in these energies, carried forward by individuals and groups. We can create such groups wherever possible, and encourage them to engage in moments of meditation or silence. If possible, we can invoke higher energies and beings in every gathering or meeting we attend, in whatever form the prevailing consciousness will allow.

The purpose of this is to instill and make practical the realization that humanity is surrounded by a vast, interdimensional community of living beings who are willing and able to provide energy and assistance whenever invited. This helps to build the foundations of understanding the great radiant sphere of lives within which humanity lives, moves and has its being.

There is also an abundance of new projects and initiatives waiting to be brought forward into human life and experience. Each awakening soul has a unique contribution to make to the plan. The synthesis and weaving of all these gifts constitute the substance of the plan on earth. This is the light substance each soul absorbs and transmits through their mental, emotional and physical/etheric bodies into the three-dimensional world.

At this time it is the key to the unfolding of the plan. The more light substance that is anchored into projects, groups, networks, and the more writing that reveals the truth of humanity's higher purpose, the more rapidly and clearly the plan will manifest. This process is accelerating as the energies intensify and more people awaken.

Revelation of the Earth's True Place in the Cosmos

Ever increasing numbers of people are having inner contact with Ashramic members and galactic beings, receiving guidance and inspiration for specific projects to fulfill, and energies to circulate and transmit to humanity and all kingdoms of nature.

These high frequency energies are becoming more easily absorbed as humanity purifies itself, reorients towards the light and opens to new inspiration about how to live in lighted and loving ways amidst massive civilizational transformation.

A significant portion of humanity now accepts that there are other advanced civilizations beyond the earth, and people are open and interested in what can be learned from them. Thus, the fundamental conditions of consciousness for galactic relationships are steadily being built, and ultimately will result in growing contact with galactic civilizations.

The energy circulation which has been seen by humanity as primarily within the sphere of earth, is rapidly expanding into its true context, with earth being seen as a chakra within the body of the Solar Being, and a member of a vast galactic family of interrelated civilizations.

These civilizations are held together by shared principles and the common purpose of advancing the development and well-being of all members of the Galactic Light Alliance. When this perspective is fully understood and integrated into human consciousness, it will be the greatest transformational event in human history.

It will be truly and completely a group awakening, revelation and initiation, made possible by the well-developed circulatory systems now in place throughout the spheres of every level of being and life on earth. This is the ultimate purpose and culmination of all the spiritual work of the past centuries — especially the last decades of building the networks of light and love and infusing them with new energies and radiating them into the human energy field.

The revelation of humanity's true place in the cosmos, and how we and the earth can collectively participate in cosmic evolution as a chakra within the body of the Solar Being, will result in our true and accurate placement of ourselves and the earth within the infinite field of Being.

It will resolve all questions about humanity's significance and the value of the individual and lighted groups and their relationship to ever larger wholes. It will be a revolution of thought and consciousness that will dwarf the Copernican revolution by a thousand times — illuminating earth's true place in the solar systemic evolution.

It will open the doorway into cosmic life and relationships for all humanity, and into a infinite future of galactic exploration and creation, all within a realized oneness with the Source/Creator. Great will be that day— it will be within our lifetimes.

Chapter 32

Immediate Next Steps
and Signs of Change

The Next Steps in the Unfolding Plan:

1. Complete the defeat of the cabal and remove them from holding any control or power;
2. Support lighted individuals and groups to take over the world systems and re-create them;
3. Provide immediate practical assistance to those in greatest need in the world;
4. Change the world atmosphere from fear and insecurity to a relaxed goodwill;
5. Provide confidence to the world's people that they will be safe, respected, provided for, and able to build creative, joyful lives.

Signs of Change: Investigations of Financial Fraud

- *UBSAG, Credit Swiss Group AG and six additional major banks* are being investigated by The Swiss Competition Commission, as the probe into the alleged manipulation of foreign exchange rates deepens.
- *Currency trading investigations are continuing,* as top executives leave and traders are suspended or fired in the face of investigations into the potential manipulation of the $5 trillion a day foreign exchange market, The New York Times reported. New York State's top financial regulator, Benjamin M. Lawsky, is investigating the Royal Bank of Scotland, Deutsche Bank and others involved in this illegal activity. The US Securities and Exchange Commission and the Commodities Futures Trading Commission are also investigating currency traders.
- *High speed stock trading abuse and insider trading* gives certain stock traders an unfair advantage over other investors. This abuse has been revealed in a new book, Flash Boys, by Michael Lewis, and as a result, investigations have been launched into this practice by the U.S. attorney general and the FBI. The FBI has also been part of a multi-year crackdown on insider trading that has led to 79 convictions of hedge fund traders and others.
- *New controls to crack down on banks are being proposed,* as there is evidence of deep-seated cultural and ethical failures at many large financial

institutions," William C. Dudley, president of the Federal Reserve Bank of New York, recently stated, according to The New York Times. These comments are based on the record of money laundering, market rigging, tax dodging, selling faulty financial products, trampling homeowner rights and rampant risk-taking which have been well documented practices of big banks and financial institutions in recent years, the Times reports. Dudley also stated they have put in place new controls to crack down on banks when they need to and they are also "putting pressure" on the boards of banks.

Positive Trends

- *The International Monetary Fund is now focusing on income inequality* in addition to its traditional concerns, according to managing director, Christine Lagard, the New York Times reported. She says that tackling inequality is part of their mandate, which is financial stability. "Anything that is likely to rock the boat financially and macroeconomically is within our mandate."

  The IMF's research has shown that income inequality makes growth less durable in most countries. A flatter distribution of income, the study concluded, contributes more to sustainable economic growth than politics, foreign debt, openness to trade, foreign investment, or its exchange rate.

- *The secret to human flourishing is the development of every individual*, the Dalai Lama recently affirmed at a two-day meeting of the conservative American Enterprise Institute. He also said free enterprise is a useful tool, but wielding capitalism for good requires deep moral awareness, according to the New York Times. He stated that money per se is not evil, but that the key question is "whether we utilize our favorable circumstances such as our good health or wealth, in positive ways, in helping others."

  Arthur C. Brooks, The president of the Institute, was obviously profoundly affected by the Dalai Lama's ideas and presence. He wrote in an op-ed piece for the Times, "Washington needs more people like the Dalai Lama, and we need practical policies based on moral empathy. Tackling these issues may offend entrenched interests, but this is immaterial, it must be done. And temporary political discomfort pales in comparison with the suffering that vulnerable people bear every day," he wrote.

- *Former U.S. President Bill Clinton spoke about galactic civilizations* on the Jimmy Kimmel show in the U.S. Clinton is one of the leaders of the Light Alliance, and knows some aspects of the plan and is aware of the galactic civilizations. "If we were visited some day, I wouldn't be surprised. There are just too many planets in the universe to think otherwise," Clinton said. His statements on television are part of preparing humanity for the revelations of the disclosure process.

- *The U.S. military plans to reduce the U.S. Army* to its smallest force since before World War II, U.S. Defense Secretary Chuck Hagel said, and take it off the war footing adopted after 9/11.

- *Russia will not import GMO products*, the country's Prime Minister Dmitry Medvedev said, adding that the nation has enough space and resources to produce organic food. Moscow has no reason to encourage the production of genetically modified products or import them into the country, Medvedev told a congress of deputies from rural settlements.

- *Finland is the first country to meet the Kyoto Accord goals in greenhouse gas emissions reduction.* Finland emissions in a five-year period of 2008-2012 were five per cent below the assigned amount of emissions specified for Finland.

Meditation on Unblocking Media Channels

- Begin your meditation by aligning your heart and soul to higher spiritual Sources, to the Angels, Masters, Shamballa and the Galactics, and see spiritual energy pouring down into the media of the world.

- Visualize the network of communications of all types, especially television, films, the internet, etc., as a vast web transmitting information, often distorted and darkened by wrong motives.

- See the entire communications web of the planet being flooded by light, love and power flowing from the meditation alignment.

- See it sweeping away all darkness, blockages and controls which might distort the light of truth reaching humanity.

- See the control of these systems flowing to lighted individuals and groups who seek to raise human consciousness into its true dynamic, creative functioning, aware of its cosmic relationships and dedicated to the good of all life on the planet.

- See the energies of Shamballa, and the spiritual Masters to flow through this web, freeing up the circulation of lighted energies, inspiring those working in the media with new, creative ideas to help enlighten and educate humanity.

- Know this work is a major contribution to the plan, and an essential part of what is needed now. Do this meditation as often as you can.

Soul Groups and Anchoring the Plan

Chapter 33

Soul Groups

In the passage of time, many events occur in the life of humanity that are not visible to most people. These include the incoming waves of various soul groups with specific purposes, such as to:

- Break through crystallized civilizational patterns
- Embody compassion and unity
- Create new social forms such as the internet and social networking
- Resist and break the power of totalitarian regimes
- Anchor spiritual energies on earth through new patterns of energy flows

In all of these, the source of major outer impacts and changes on earth are to be found in the soul group which emanates from the inner worlds with a specific, unified purpose and task. These are carried out with varying degrees of alignment with the pure, originating impulse. Each of these groups contributes to evolutionary progress. Much of the current upheaval on earth is due to the vast number of soul groups who have simultaneously incarnated to assist in the transfiguration of the earth at this crucial time.

Each generation has brought in a new wave, carrying powerful transformative energies, building upon the previous progress from earlier waves. There has been no pause between these dynamic impulses carried by each soul group, as each succeeding wave is responding to ever-increasing frequencies of cosmic and galactic energies with greater power and precision.

This progression is facilitated by the increasing potency in materializing all the spiritual energies and plans seeking to enter the earth and affect humanity's consciousness and way of life. Tremendous leaps of consciousness and understanding are occurring with unprecedented speed in science and spirituality, as well as in fields such as ethics in the financial world. Once the cabal is removed, this will accelerate very rapidly, allowing the plan to more fully guide human civilization.

Identifying Your Soul Group

To contribute to the outworking of the Divine plan, it is useful for each individual to reflect upon the soul group which you feel most aligned and identified with. These groups include:

- Lighted Political Activators
- New Civilization Builders

- Financial Guardians
- Transformational Artists
- Energetic Healers
- Soul Inspired Teachers
- Scientific Synthesizers
- Technology Transformers
- Creative Magicians

These symbolic designations can help light workers find the right placement for their field of activity and creation, attract co-creative partners, and focus their energies with their true soul group. Standing shoulder to shoulder, with hearts and minds as one, each can then maximize their individual creativity and contribution within their soul group.

Each of the soul groups is a different and unique pathway of service and connection to the plan. Every field of endeavor can be connected to the plan once the individual or group has a clear understanding of how the plan is unfolding.

This is why it is important that the vision of humanity's unfolding future is clearly presented and held by as many people as possible. The plan is meant to permeate the consciousness of humanity and be consciously held by a majority, and ultimately by all people, with each individual understanding on their own level.

For ordinary people, the plan will mean having a good life, raising a family in a loving, cooperative community, and being creatively expressive in their lives. For those who seek to serve in larger arenas, there will be a multitude of opportunities to organize society in harmonious and loving ways through business, politics, education, etc.

For those with an expanded consciousness and a worldwide view, there can be leadership and creativity on an international level. For others, the greatest service will be to connect with galactic civilizations and build relationships with these civilizations beyond the earth. Each will serve in the arena that corresponds to their level of consciousness and developed capacities.

When all the soul groups are working consciously within a true understanding of the plan of transfiguration, the evolutionary progress of humanity will seem miraculous in the speed of transformation and the improvement in the worldwide human condition.

This is why it is useful to help each advanced soul know and understand who their true co-creative soul partners are. Drawing them together through resonance of purpose and vibrational frequency, and working in harmony and joy for the good of the whole is the goal. This is how the plan is being fulfilled.

Divine Understanding and a Completed Point of View

Divine understanding is seeing clearly how all events, circumstances and situations lead eventually to the fulfillment of the Divine plan. Although there may be delays in the plan, all that occurs ultimately leads to a deeper understanding and wisdom in humanity, and in the end fulfills the plan.

Divine understanding is also fully appreciating and utilizing the multidimensional nature of reality and the Great Chain of Being as an organizing principle. This is a recognition that each level of being is held in love within a greater being, in an infinite series of nested hierarchies.

A completed point of view means understanding the multiple factors present in each set of circumstances — the actors, the timing and the process of unfoldment; constant change and adaptation; and the ultimate goals of the Solar and Planetary Beings.

Patience and acceptance of the rightness of all that occurs is required, even though it may seem that the whole world is in limbo or chaos while waiting for the plan to unfold. This is partially true, and yet much activity is happening beneath the surface, and as energy is unblocked to support the plan, all will be revealed.

Chapter 34

The Transformational Tipping Point

In order for the plan to be brought to completion for the current cycle, there must be a sufficient inflow and anchoring of light to shift the balance with the dark lodge. Humanity and the Light Alliance has approached this point several times before, and each time the dark forces have found ways to instill fear, lower consciousness, and create a contraction of the light.

However, this time such actions are no longer possible, as any such initiatives are being contained and completely stopped by the Light Alliance, including assistance from the Galactics. For this reason, we are about to reach the transformational tipping point where the light out balances the dark.

This will open the revelation of Oneness, Divine love, and the necessary actions to completely delegitimize and remove the cabal from power. These steps can and will be taken, implemented by the vast field of light workers on many different dimensions. This is a new condition, as the resistances and blockages to the flow and circulation of light are melting away, and all attempts to reestablish these blockages are being removed.

The Pressure Wave on the Cabal

What about all the evidence of dark activity by major corporations and power elites, which has not dissipated? It may seem that there is a massive lobbying against any good or decent idea to help humanity, and the political games are endless.

The activity of the dark side has not been fully shut down, nor will it be until the Day of Revelation and the months following. But on the deeper, causal level, the inflowing, all-permeating light is building up a tremendous pressure wave that is keeping the dark forces from doing anything major to harm humanity or the planet at this time.

It is also weakening the dark forces' control, as they are forced to spend more and more time, energy and money defending against the inflowing light, which is bringing their activities and control systems into the light of public scrutiny.

As this wave of pressure continues to build, the light forces have more and more energetic support to expose the workings of the cabal, to connect and join together in new alliances, and continue building the new civilization with increased power and inner support. This is happening all around the planet and is the guarantee of ultimate victory. The numbers of people working with lighted groups and projects is rapidly increasing every day.

The revelations about the manipulations of the financial system for individual greed is now fully anchored within most people's understanding, preparing them for a true transformation of the system, as outlined here. The plan to have banks reorganized as public utilities, with interest-free money backed by gold and commodities, and distribution of the cabal's money for all of humanity, is fully prepared and awaiting the time for activation.

Chapter 35

The Meaning of Crop Circles

The increasing appearance of unidentified lights over many cities, especially at night, are a well-documented phenomenon. Crop circles, the beautiful geometric patterns mysteriously appearing in crop fields all over the world in recent years, especially in Britain, are key messages from the Galactics. Crop circles are created by galactic ships, using small, mobile projecting devices that are designed to create intricate patterns with deep cosmic meaning. Some of these have been partially deciphered by investigators who understand they are symbolic messages from very advanced civilizations.

A significant new crop circle appeared on June 6, 2014 during a gathering of world leaders who met in Normandy, France to commemorate the 70th anniversary of the Normandy beach landing on D day, which led to the liberation of Europe from Nazi domination. This was a very significant gathering during which many plans for the implementation of the worldwide financial reorganization were discussed and agreed to by world leaders.

The new crop circle appeared in Chilcomb Down, near Winchester in Hampshire in the United Kingdom. These symbols in the circle were in Morse code, which upon analysis gave the very clear message, "No More War." For those who understand the deeper meaning of this event, it was clear that the Galactics were signaling their support of the planning and implementation of the new system for the world.

The crop circles are part of the plan to awaken humanity to the reality of galactic civilizations, who are non-hostile and seeking to communicate with humanity and make their presence known. This has been a successful endeavor, and has led millions of people to be more open to the presence of galactic life around earth.

Combined with the accelerated visibility of spacecraft in the skies day and night all over the world, humanity is steadily opening to the truth of benevolent galactic beings, despite all the propaganda of the cabal. Humanity is being prepared for the disclosure of these galactic civilizations, some time following the Day of Revelation. All is unfolding in Divine law and order.

Chapter 36

Anchoring the Plan

There are many facets of the plan which are very complex and will require time to implement. Transforming the energy basis for the entire civilization, including electricity, transportation and industrial use will require setting up manufacturing and installation of new free energy devices which draw energy directly from the etheric planes. This will be done with the greatest possible speed, once the cabal is removed and humanity understands the plan and what it means for human life and the earth.

Healthcare and medical treatments will be radically transformed with healing chambers, DNA enhancement and multidimensional energetic approaches. Schools will be established to train doctors and medical personnel, as well as educating the public in these new, advanced healing modalities. The teachers in these schools will be members of the Light Alliance. Some will be Galactics, although they will initially be occupying human forms, to be more acceptable to humanity.

Education will be revised to teach current humanity and the next generation of incoming souls the true history of earth, the reality of galactic civilizations, the multidimensional constitution of the human being, and the possibilities open to all for soul growth and expression. Inventors and builders will be given information and blueprints for many new technologies to enhance human well-being, and will be assisted in improving upon them with creative human ideas.

New forms of art, music and creative expression will unfold to celebrate a human consciousness which is capable of moving with grace and ease through multiple dimensions, opening a vast new field of expression and beauty to be enjoyed and interacted with.

All these developments will be the result of the great revelations of Oneness and the many dimensions of life which have been previously inaccessible to humanity. The world will be in a state of consciousness and being which is inconceivable from the current prevailing consciousness. The new world will inevitably unfold from the waves of light, love and cosmic energies breaking upon the shores of human awareness like a golden tide, revealing a sunrise of indescribable splendor.

Developments in the Economy and Financial System

- *132 nations want out of the cabal banking system*, reports *Nation of Change*. These nations, who are part of the G77 Coalition (one of the largest coalitions of developing nations in history) have urged Secretary General of the United Nations, Ban Ki-moon, to provide, "as soon as possible...alternative options for banking services." This comes on the heels of a mass cancellation of bank accounts in U.N. missions and those of foreign US diplomats. The G77 urged the Secretary General to review the "U.N. Secretariat's financial relations with the J.P. Morgan Chase Bank and consider alternatives to such financial institutions and to report thereon, along with the information requested." The 77 member countries expressed a "deep concern" over the decisions made by several other banking institutions, including JP Morgan Chase, in closing bank accounts for mostly developing countries.

- *U.S. Attorney General signals criminal charges coming against some banks*, according to the *Bloomberg News*. It reported that U.S. Attorney General Eric Holder and his department is readying criminal cases against banks that show financial institutions aren't too big to prosecute. Holder said improved coordination with regulators is creating a relationship that "will prove key in the coming weeks and months" as prosecutors pursue charges. The government is nearing decisions on whether to charge Credit Suisse Group AG (CSGN) and BNP Paribas SA, people familiar with those probes said.

- *Banks are being sued on claims of fixing the price of gold*, and accusations of collusion among five banks that set the price of gold two times each day have now been filed in Federal District Court in Manhattan, according to the New York Times. The five banks — Barclays, Scotia Bank, Deutsche Bank, HSBC and Society Generale — are accused of collusion by trading on the price of gold before publication of the new gold price to the wider market.

Galactic Contact

- *ET's making themselves known on mainstream media* according to a new video compilation which offers a wonderful (yet, no doubt miniscule) synthesis of some of the U.S. mainstream media coverage of recent UFO sightings. The video was published on YouTube on May 10, 2014 by AlienPeace1, with an article entitled "There is GOOD Out There" that says:

    "UFOs have been appearing in our skies for thousands of years.

But now something new is happening. Orbs of light in a triangle formation are repeatedly appearing over major cities all over the world. Because they always make a triangle, it is clear they are intelligently controlled, and not any sort of freely floating objects.

"So if these orbs of light are in fact extra-terrestrial, why are they appearing above our major population centers? If they were merely observing us for scientific reasons, then surely they could do so without us seeing them. Yet they repeatedly appear as huge, bright lights in a clear triangle formation. It seems as if they want us to see them and are trying to wake us up to the fact that we are not alone in the Universe. And perhaps this is their way of initiating contact.

"But if they want to make us aware that we are not alone, and make contact with us, then why don't they just land? Well, what would happen if a giant spaceship suddenly landed on the White House lawn? How would we react to that? How would the military react? How would the media react? Bright lights in the sky are very non-threatening. And it isn't immediately obvious what they are. In takes some figuring out. And in the process of figuring it out, we have time to absorb the reality of it. We have time to process the shock and fear.

"They are initiating contact, but in a way that doesn't shock and terrify us. These beings clearly understand our psychology very well, and are showing great sensitivity to our emotions. They know what they are doing. Right now at this time, they are observing how we are reacting. They are waiting for us to figure it out. And waiting to see if and how we respond to them." To see the video go to:

http://goldenageofgaia.com/2014/05/18/video-ets-making-themselves-known-on-mainstream-media/

Good News in the Energy Sector:

- *Electric Cars receive 'stellar' reliability report from Consumer's Union*, as electric cars are proving that simpler is better, a recent Consumer Reports owner survey has concluded. "In general, electric cars have been stellar," says Jake Fisher, director of auto testing for Consumer's Union. "The fact that they don't have to carry around a gas engine or conventional transmission tends to make them pretty reliable." In Norway, electric cars outsold all other models of traditional fuel cars the last three months of 2013.
- *Obama recently announced actions on renewable energy*, including steps to increase the use of solar panels, boost energy efficiency in federal buildings and train more people to work in the renewable energy field,

Reuters reported. "It's the right thing to do for the planet," Obama said, speaking at a WalMart store that features roof-top solar panels and a charging station for electric vehicles, among other energy-saving retrofits. The president showed how major corporations have committed to increasing the generation of solar power at their facilities. Wal-Mart Stores, Apple, Yahoo, Google and Ikea are among the companies that have made such commitments.

Environmental Sensitivity and Protection

- *Millions march against Monsanto and GMOS on May 24, 2014*, protesting the GMO (genetically modified organisms) giant company. The march simultaneously took place in more than 400 cities in 52 countries that span six continents. That's up from 286 cities in 36 countries last year. "Historically, Monsanto has brought us DDT, PCBs, Agent Orange and dioxin," reads a Facebook invitation to the march, as reported in EcoWatch. "Monsanto's reckless use of chemicals calls into question their testing standards, lack of scientific rigor, disregard for the precautionary principle and disregard for human life and the ecosystem.

  "Currently, we're faced with Monsanto's seed patenting and subsequent extortion in demanding pay for seeds from future crops, the proliferation of genetically modified foods (GMOs), use of dangerous pesticides, and their efforts to control the food supply. Monsanto leaves damaged farms, people, animals and entire ecosystems in their wake. Monsanto's harmful practices are causing soil infertility, mono-cropping, loss of biodiversity, habitat destruction and contributing to beehive collapse. GMO crops cross pollenate with traditional crops, risking peasant farmers' livelihood."

- *India declares dolphins "non-human persons,"* and India's Ministry of Environment and Forests has agreed to ban the use of dolphins, whales and porpoises for public entertainment and to prevent them from being held captive anywhere in India according to Positive News. The ministry said "cetaceans in general are highly intelligent and sensitive, and scientists studying dolphins have suggested that their unusually high intelligence as compared to other animals means dolphins should be seen as 'non—human persons' and should have their own specific rights."

- *In China, 64 percent say they are environmentalists*, which is more than double that of Europe and the United States, a report by Reuters recently showed. The survey by a Dutch research agency said in China, where public anger has mounted over hazardous levels of pollution in towns and cities, environmentalists had a greater sense of urgency about action needed to tackle the problem than Western counterparts, where the financial crisis has knocked environmental policy down the political agenda.

• *New pollution-fighting billboards can purify 100,000 cubic meters of air every day* according to the University of Engineering and Technology of Peru (UTEC) which is on a mission to transform regular billboards into structures that tackle environmental issues. Following the success of their billboard that converts humidity into drinkable water, the team has developed pollution-fighting billboards that can purify 100,000 cubic meters of air every day, according to a report in Global Good News.

Section X

Infusing Atomic Light
into Our DNA

Chapter 37

Galactic Alignments, Photons and DNA

The evolution of life and consciousness on earth has proceeded through long eons to reach a culminating point at this time. This is the time for lifting the dark veils from the planet imposed by the dark forces, leading to the full infusion of light into the earth and humanity, which is the transfiguration of earth.

Each realm of planets, solar systems and galaxies are affected by changes in cosmic alignments and the resulting new energies released into the solar systems and planets contained within them.

The entrance of our galaxy into what scientists call the photon band over the past 20 years, as well as ever growing light from the galactic civilizations, has contributed to the increase in light flowing into our solar system and earth. Not only is earth being fed by greater light, but the consciousness of each individual is being infused with a greater purity and potency of light, contributing to purification, awakening, and increasing capacity to hold and use this light.

Earth has two poles, just as we do, with the north as the positive pole and the south as the receptive pole. It is the balance of the dynamic and attractive energies inflowing and circulating in a toroidal field around the earth which holds the form of earth in balance.

Through the study of the movement of light, scientists have named photons as the quantifiable bundle of energy that moves through time and space at a predictable speed of 186,000 miles per second.

Photons do not register as having mass in the three dimensions; however they have great effects on higher etheric, astral and mental dimensions. Through their velocity, they function as a wave to transfer energy to other energetic fields.

Thus there are no particles — all is energy. Ultimately, photons are successive waves of light with a cyclic rhythm, but they can condense or function as particles in the lower frequency energy fields, based on how humans perceive the light.

Light, as waves or as photons, is essential to all life on earth. Humans need it for intelligent activity, animals for vitality and activity, plants for photosynthesis, and minerals for radiation. Light, taken into your human energetic and organic system, distributes electromagnetic frequencies to all systems in your body, including the nucleus of each molecule where the DNA is located.

DNA then radiates light throughout your body between all levels, down to communication between cells. This light transfer brings higher intelligence, wisdom and spiritual will into your body, heart, mind and soul.

Science is Proving We Are Made of Light

Experiments using a new technology are showing that a biophoton or Ultra-weak Photon Emission, (UPE) is a kind of light particle that is emitted by all living things. These can be captured and stored inside of cells and can travel through our nervous system; suggesting that biophotons might provide a way for cells to transfer energy and communicate information. It's has also been suggested that UPEs might even have properties which help us to visualize images. Today, our computers transmit electrical information which is a form of light. Now our sciences are revealing humans work the same way, and light carries information through our brain and nervous system.

As reported in *Spirit Science,* scientists are finding that our DNA is a strong source of UPEs, and it communicates with and is created from light itself. Scientists have also discovered that not only do we emit light, we have the ability to affect it with our thoughts. In a recent study, participants were placed in a darkened room and asked to visualize a bright light. When they did this, they were able to increase their levels of biophoton emissions significantly, proving that our intentions have an influence on light itself.

Transmitting Atomic Light to Your DNA

Until very recently, scientists have viewed DNA as a fixed mechanism. This is because of their tendency to regard the mechanisms and systems of human beings as fixed and unchanging, and because they do not understand the nature of the life of our physical form as an evolutionary unfoldment.

The discovery (called *epigenetics*) that mind, emotions and consciousness actually can change the structure and activity of DNA has yet to fully permeate scientific thinking. However, as spiritual scientists, we know from the wisdom teachings about the tremendous transfigurational potential of higher frequency atomic light and its activating effect on DNA. This is a major step beyond current scientific understanding.

It is possible for us as awakened individuals to construct a pathway for invoking higher atomic light into our etheric/vital energy system and to radiate that light to our DNA, raising its frequency. This activates and opens DNA, resulting in new capacities for us.

DNA thrives and grows with increased light and diminishes when light is lacking. Scientists measure light in photons or degrees of brightness. What they are actually measuring is the degree of atomic substance present within the light.

Atomic substance is higher frequency energy from higher subplanes (defined on next page). Scientists are actually measuring the degree of this light present in the etheric energy body, although they are unaware of the source of this light.

Once contact with atomic light substance is made, received and absorbed, it can be distributed to the DNA consciously by the awakened individual. This is most effectively done by visualizing the DNA present in your entire body, and seeing the double DNA spiral and the genes being filled with light circulating up and down the spiral.

(Please see the meditation following this discussion.)

Circulating Light to Poles of DNA

It is important to understand that one pole of your body and your DNA is the positive Spirit pole and the other is the receptive Matter pole. The key to balanced energy circulation is to see energy entering in the Spirit pole and exiting from the Matter pole and then returning upward to rejoin the Spirit pole. We see this energy movement displayed very clearly in the double helix of DNA strands.

To bring in atomic light, you simply need to ask your soul and Spirit to bring in the appropriate level of atomic light for the next step in your evolution.

In the meditation you will first bring down this atomic light in a clockwise spiral, through all your bodies and then circulate it back up in a counterclockwise direction to the Spirit source, and then repeat this flow with your tiny DNA strands, thus shifting from the macrocosm to the microcosm.

We will include visualizing this atomic light circulation within the DNA of each molecule, coming down clockwise into the DNA, all the way to its base, then reversing direction, moving upwards counterclockwise through the DNA spiral to the Spirit pole, source of the atomic light.

Done in this way, a balance is maintained between the Spirit and Matter poles within your being, and the work can be done safely and most effectively.

Planes and Subplanes

To understand how DNA affects your whole organism, you need to understand planes and subplanes. Planes are different fields of energy at different frequencies, all contained within the cosmic physical plane, which is the field within which we are functioning.

There are seven planes: the physical/etheric, astral (emotional), mental, buddhic (intuitional), atmic (will), cosmic and logoic. Each of these are divided into seven subplanes, totaling 49 subplanes in all.

DNA is located on the first or highest subplane of the etheric, (the vital body which energizes your physical body) and has corresponding resonances to the first subplanes of the astral/emotional and mental worlds. There are energetic connections between each of the subplanes of your etheric, astral and mental bodies. This is how changes in DNA can affect your entire energetic system.

The Results of Infusing DNA with Atomic Light

As higher subplanes are activated, this activates perception, energetic circulation and expanding capacities on each of the lesser frequency subplanes. Consciousness then expands into a fuller functioning on each of these subplanes.

This means that as the DNA is activated with higher frequency atomic light, you have increased ability to perceive and use more and more subtle physical, emotional, mental and spiritual capacities such as:

- Physically, you have greater strength, endurance and vitality to radiate to others through your energetic/vital body;
- Emotionally, your range and subtlety expand, with increased emotional power and influence as well as greater empathy, compassion and subtle emotional sensitivity;
- Mentally, you have an increase in the range, speed, flexibility and power of your thought, resulting in an expanded capacity for creative thought and increased mental influence;
- Spiritually, you have greater intuition, foresight, telepathy and greater capacity to uplift and transform others, with deep perception into causes and subtle levels of the One Life, including contact with higher beings.

Meditation on Infusing Your DNA with Atomic Light

- Take a few deep breaths, breathing in peace and stillness, and relax. Breathe out any thoughts or concerns and let everything go. Bring your attention fully into the present moment, letting go of the past, letting go of the future.

- Focus in your heart, and see a radiant sun of light and love in your heart, filling you with positive, sunlight energy.

- Invite your soul to bring more love and light into that sun center in your heart.

- Now radiate light and love from the sun in your heart down towards your solar plexus center in your belly, the seat of your subconscious, seeing it filled with the warmth and light of love.

- Appreciate and be grateful to your subconscious for all it does to help and support you.

- Invite your subconscious to bring the sunlight and love in your solar plexus up into your heart.

- Now see energy rising upward through your central channel, connecting with a greater sun above your head, the sun of Soul/Spirit, which is the source of atomic light.

- See these three lights — above your head, in your heart and in your solar plexus, each radiating its light and love to the others.

- Now ask your soul/Spirit to radiate to you the perfect degree and frequency of atomic light for your next step in your evolution.

- See this atomic light spiraling down around you clockwise, filling your mental, emotional and etheric physical bodies with light.

- Then see it spiraling counterclockwise back up to the soul/Spirit sun above you. Allow this flow to continue for a few moments.

- Now see the same down flowing spiral of light pour into a strand of your DNA, as an archetype of all the DNA strands in your cells.

- Again see this atomic light coming down from your soul/Spirit, spiraling down clockwise and entering in through the Spirit pole of your DNA and exiting from the Matter pole, and then spiraling counterclockwise upwards through your DNA, through the Spirit pole and back to the light above your head.

- Allow this flow to continue with one strand of DNA until you understand exactly how the energy is flowing.

- Now visualize all the billions of DNA double spirals in the nucleus of each cell in your entire body.

- See the light flowing into all of them from the Spirit pole to the Matter pole, and from there counterclockwise back up to the Spirit pole. See all the billions of DNA strands in your body being lighted up as this light flows in.

- See this light bathing your DNA in higher atomic light, cleansing, purifying and filling your DNA strands with light, raising their frequency, activating your DNA and adding new capacities and strengths to your physical, emotional and mental bodies.

- Know that this infusion of light, love and power into your vehicles will make them more responsive to soul love, communication and higher purpose.

- Take a few moments to allow these life frequencies to permeate through all levels of your being.

Chapter 38

Energy Flows and the Purpose of Earth

Many teachers focus on moving people out of the personal/ego, because they assume people are dense and stuck in 3D. Some are too grounded, and need this intense focus to help them rise upwards. But many people are already in touch with higher energies, and may be overwhelmed by them and their impact on their physical, emotional and mental bodies.

Many of you reading this book are already in touch with higher energies to varying degrees, and need clearing and balancing to deal with the impact of these energies.

Your energy field is a double helix vortex with light flowing in both clockwise and counterclockwise directions. The left brain registers and accesses clockwise 3-D energies and the physical, emotional, and mental fields, and the right brain registers the higher, counterclockwise energies, which spiral into the spiritual dimensions.

As you reverse the spin of 3 Dimensional clockwise time to a counterclockwise spin, this expands your energy to unite with soul/Spirit. However, in using this as an energy visualization, it is important to balance this with a clockwise grounding spin to anchor the energies.

Microscopically within the atom, electrons spin clockwise when they serve the grounding function of anchoring consciousness into the material world and into physical and etheric bodies.

However, with the increasing light and raising of consciousness into the 4th and 5th dimensions, certain electrons will begin to spin counterclockwise in response to the ascending energies. Just as in the DNA strands, there needs to be a balance of ascending and descending energies.

Electrons associated with higher subplane frequencies of energy will begin to rotate counterclockwise, while some remain clockwise to keep the physical form in manifestation.

Atoms of higher subplane substance are rotating primarily counterclockwise, although some remain clockwise to hold the form of the subtle bodies in place. As you enter the denser subplanes, more atoms are rotating clockwise then counterclockwise, as less atomic substance has permeated these energetic frequencies in those dimensions.

As ascension proceeds, there are more counterclockwise rotations, but a minimum is still required to hold the form in place. The DNA is causal to the electron spin, so as you work with the DNA spin/rotation, the electrons will adjust as the DNA comes into balanced circulation in both directions.

Inner Synergy Into the Still Point

The Transfiguration process ultimately eliminates the divisions in your mind and body to reunite and balance the right and left brain into a cohesive oneness. This creates a neutral still point in the heart and brain, resulting in a coherence field and allowing the soul to descend more fully into your being.

The corpus callosum is the physical/etheric mechanism which balances the two hemispheres of the brain. The pineal and pituitary glands become active when the right and left hemispheres are infused with the right balance of light, and become active and balanced. The Universal Presence or the One Life is the origin of the still point and the unified mind. It is the larger field which you can enter from the coherent still point in your mind and heart.

Balancing the heart and mind is a similar resonating process to balancing right and left hemispheres of the brain. This includes a two-way connection between the mind and feelings, and the heart/brain synergy is the key.

The soul and Spirit play a key role in stimulating this coherence/synergy, which is why it is important to work with these levels of your being as the source point for your meditation work with atomic light.

The heart allows you to live in the Now, and the brain/mind can interpret and organize the experiences, as long as it does not take over and block the experience. With the assistance of the soul, anchored in and stimulating both the brain/mind and the heart, the heart frequency dissolves barriers of space/time into the universal quantum field, or the field of the One Life.

A Key to the Unique Purpose of Earth

The Central Sun at the galactic core is a portal to other worlds and dimensions, and also the gate for inflowing energies from other galactic civilizations and the Galactics themselves.

One of the factors in the Transfiguration is understanding the function of silica in the unfoldment of human consciousness on Earth. Silica has certain transmitting properties because it can hold energy, and then release it in appropriate pulses to transmit information.

It is the basis of the silicon chip which has transformed modern human life and communication. Earth itself also has a high percentage of silica/quartz in its geological makeup, and thus the planet as a whole has the capacity to receive and transmit energy.

This is the key to its ultimate purpose, which is to be a receiving, storage and transmitting station for higher energies from many dimensions and galaxies and then transmitting these to the entire solar system and galaxy.

Humanity is intended to develop the capacity to link with the galactic communications network through frequency attunement with the soul and higher spiritual contacts. These pathways of communication between the soul and the embodied self are built by linking the pineal and pituitary (third eye) chakra with higher intelligence.

Power points and sacred sites have a higher concentration of quartz/silica, and are utilized by higher spiritual beings as places where human telepathic capacities can more easily link with them. Light then pours in, is anchored in these sites, and builds up an energetic field which remains and grows with human contact with these sources of higher energies.

Likewise, in human beings, the increase in light/photons stimulates a connection with higher intelligences and expanded contact with higher worlds. The liquid crystal light of photons vibrates at a higher frequency, and links us to these higher beings and truths.

You can amplify this by using quartz crystals in your meditation work, but most important is the work to purify your consciousness, think along higher lines, and practice compassion for all beings.

Chapter 39

Ascension Symptoms and Managing Overstimulation

As you purify your energetic field and bodies, open to higher energies and consciously invoke higher frequency light and love, there is an intense stimulation of your physical, emotional and mental bodies, which can lead to what are called "ascension symptoms".

This is a natural step in the purification process, and will bring to the surface many hidden and denser energies for transmutation, transformation and ultimately transfiguration.

All these processes can cause a variety of uncomfortable conditions, but there are many things you can do to help minimize these difficulties. Knowing that this is a natural part of the process helps to relieve anxiety that you may have a serious illness. When you experience any of these symptoms take time for extra rest, high quality food and water, and relaxation.

These symptoms can include: body aches and pains; difficulty in focusing your mind; skin rashes; low-grade fevers and exhaustion; sudden food or chemical sensitivities; high sensitivity to crowds, sounds, light, sunlight; dizziness or nausea; heart palpitations, and electrical-like vibrations or buzzing.

Balancing Ascending and Descending Energies

Here are some specific action steps and adjustments you can do to best maintain your Spirit/matter balance during the transmutation/transfiguration process:

- Clarify which of your subconscious parts hold heavier, blocking energies, discover their limiting views and attitudes and link them with your soul. Help them make a free will choice to change these obstructing patterns.
- Strive to maintain positive thoughts about what is occurring and where it is leading you at all times. See whatever occurs as a purification and recalibration of your entire system and bodies.
- Moderate your meditations if you have too much energy flowing in.
- Practice group meditations whenever possible, as this helps to balance and circulate energy, (as long as the meditations are not too intensive).
- Contemplate and hold a vision for the upliftment of humanity and all

life on our planet, seeing a world which allows people to live in freedom, creativity and joy.

- Share love, compassion and your gifts with others, as this is a powerful way to ground spiritual energies and create joyful states of consciousness.
- Include positive emotional expression and enjoyment with friends and family, listening to uplifting music, being in nature, and focusing on what allows your heart to open and expand with joy.
- Fill your mind with positive, lighted and inspiring ideas, and engage in conversations with those who can function on a positive mental level.
- Nurture your physical/etheric body with healthy food that is filled with life force, grown nearby and free of artificial additives.
- Allow plenty of time in nature with fresh air, sunshine, an abundance of living plants and pure oxygen.
- Exercise in nature to circulate pure life force through your physical/etheric body.
- Get plenty of sleep and minimize insomnia by avoiding excessive food, reading on computers or e-books, and other mentally and emotionally stimulating activities before retiring.
- Be sure your room is completely dark at night with no light entering.
- Focus on higher spiritual centers such as the Ashram of Synthesis or great spiritual beings who inspire you, as you enter the sleep state.
- Ask to remember your dreams, if you like, so that you can bring back whatever positive teaching or experiences you have while out of your body.

Grounding and Lowering Your Frequency

There may be times when your process becomes so intense that you feel overcharged and overloaded with energy. You may experience headaches, jitteriness, inability to focus, dizziness or other symptoms of excessive stimulation.

The foundational principle in dealing with this condition is to remember that you are a circulation system with flows throughout all your bodies. Health and balance results from a full circulation of energies on the physical/etheric, emotional, mental and spiritual levels of your being. Here is what you can do if you are excessively stimulated and need to temporarily lower your frequency:

- Reduce or minimize your meditations for a period of time and then use shorter, more heart-centered meditations until you feel more in balance.
- Ground your energy by walking barefoot on the earth whenever possible, dancing, and taking salt baths.

- It has been proven that direct bare skin contact with the Earth removes excessive positive electrons in your body and replaces them with beneficial negative electrons of the earth, bringing your body into balance and harmony.
- This is why walking on the sand along the ocean is so peaceful, relaxing and rejuvenating. If it is not possible to do this, put your bare feet on the earth somewhere, preferably where there is dampness in the earth.
- Eat foods that strengthen your root/base chakra when necessary, which includes all root vegetables (and meat if you are so inclined).
- Drink wine or eat anything with sugar, which will immediately lower your frequency. (This is not recommended as a long-term practice).
- Connect with animals, plants and minerals by having their energy around you.
- Use massage and bodywork when needed, especially foot massages, reflexology and energetic balancing treatments to keep your system in a good circulatory flow.

Chapter 40

Updates on the Plan
and The Great Rejoicing

There is now a clarity of agreement within the Light Alliance on moving forward to complete the removal of the cabal. All the arrangements have been made, agreements signed, and the members await the moment of the release of the transforming energy, which will occur when humanity is ready to receive it. This is the intense wave of love and powerful light from the Solar Being which will lift all those ready into the new state of consciousness and being.

When this begins, it is important for as many people as possible to understand what is happening and why, so that false information is neutralized. As previously stated, the Light Alliance will take over the media, which may take a few days to be implemented. During this period, the financial reorganization will begin.

It is important for people to understand the depth and breadth of what is occurring so they have patience and willingness to allow the process to unfold before panicking and making superficial assessments. Even people who love to offer their biased opinions about everything will ultimately be overwhelmed by the positive evidence.

The primary attitude people need to hold is a positive expectancy that a vast revelatory change is taking place on the planet, and that this will culminate in revealing the truth of earth's history, the true place of humanity and earth within cosmic evolution, and the positive future for earth and all lives upon her.

Those who have been opposed to the evolutionary flow will be gone from earth, moved to other dimensions appropriate for them. This is because of the intensity of the energy that will be flowing in, and the decisions the dark ones have made to resist evolution. We can trust the benevolence of the Universe in this process.

Of course, it is understandable that people would be afraid and suspicious after all the cabal has done to humanity. And yet, through the cabal's overreaching for total control, they have unintentionally awakened people and stimulated revolt. Humanity will not accept the status quo any longer, which is the necessary prerequisite for all these changes to occur.

Indicators of Current Progress

- *President Obama is pointing the way forward in fulfilling the plan* of the Light Alliance with initiatives on climate change through reduction of carbon emissions, efforts to resolve the immigration issue in the U.S., increased taxes on the wealthy to be distributed to less well-off families, preserving internet neutrality, and protecting pristine areas of wilderness and oceans in the United States.

- *Faith Leaders Declare Slavery a Crime Against Humanity*, including Pope Francis, Justin Welby, the Archbishop of Canterbury and Head of the Anglican Church, Amma, Mata Amritanandamayi, and many other leaders of the world's religions came together in one voice to declare that modern slavery is a crime against humanity. They called on all people, irrespective of gender, faith and culture, to work together to eradicate human trafficking and all other forms of slavery from the face of the Earth by 2020.

- *The annual Edelman Trust Barometer Report*, a 27-country survey measuring confidence in the public and private sectors, found that the majority of the world's people think technology change is moving too fast for them. By 2 to 1, people believe that governments or businesses are not thinking enough about the broad societal impact of social media, digital security, genetically modified foods and fracking. Technology for technology's sake, most people feel, is not a good thing. This is very good news as it shows that the general public is more and more aware of the harmful and controlling aspects of the cabal's activities around the world.

- *The Sharing Economy* has emerged as a major challenge to traditional corporate businesses. There are now over 10,000 companies in the sharing economy, allowing people to run their own transportation services, hotels, restaurants, kennels, and yard equipment rental services.

   "All over the world people are turning to one another to build the type of economy we want to see," said Natalie Foster of peers.org. "We're sharing our homes, cars, skills, time and money, building babysitting cooperatives and new ways of carpooling," Foster said. "We are rejecting the idea that stuff makes us happier and that ownership is better than access. We're building a movement where access trumps ownership."

   This explosion of the sharing economy is based on discovering that although we may distrust strangers, we totally trust people —significantly more than we trust corporations or governments. The key is having both the provider and user rate each other. As people learn to trust and cooperate with each other for their mutual benefit, they are overcoming the sense of isolation and separation and as some have said, it even has "restored their faith in humanity."

• *Meditation for children and young adults in classrooms* programs worldwide are showing remarkable results. Fourth and fifth graders who participated in a mindfulness meditation and kindness program showed better social skills and were better liked. Mindful meditators had math cores that were 15% higher than their peers. In the UK, British children 12 to 16 who were given nine lessons in a mindfulness program had lower depression scores, less stress and better well-being.

Expansion of the Light Alliance and Our Highest Stance Now

All is unfolding in Divine order and the Light Alliance is gaining strength and depth, with new allies joining every day. More and more individuals and organizations within the financial system are joining forces with the Light Alliance to transform and reset the financial system. Each has their idea about what this entails, but as they come into the orbit of the Light Alliance their vision is expanded, and they are brought into alignment with the plan. This is how the outcome is being assured.

There are few people who do not realize that major change is occurring in the world with more to come. Some are self-preserving, some are frozen in place, and some are adapting and opening to the new possibilities. All will be swept along in the current of events as they unfold.

The best way to prepare for the Day of Revelation is to organize your life to eliminate all unnecessary pulls on your consciousness, all old preoccupations which are of a lower frequency, and instead focus on what lifts your vibration into the higher positive dimensions of consciousness and being.

Standing in the future, living it as your reality now, and helping others to do so, is the essential way you can contribute to the new world. You can experience the maximized flow of love energy as you transcend time and live in this future reality now.

The Day of Revelation will be an even greater collective experience of love, as the resistance from the darker frequencies will be removed, so all who are ready can move into higher consciousness.

As for practical preparations, there will be no disruptions in supply lines, and the financial system will be reset very rapidly, so there is no need for concern about your physical needs.

Since the control of the media will shift on the Day of Revelation and will be part of a coordinated action, accurate, true information on what is occurring will be available to all.

Free Will and the Timing of the Day of Revelation

As mentioned earlier, because free will and the readiness and supportive activity of human consciousness are key factors in implementing the Day of Revelation, the timing is not fixed. However, due to the plans and decrees of the Solar Being, the plan will be implemented within a reasonable time cycle for the well-being of humanity and the larger system.

In order to accelerate this process, every light worker's greatest contribution is the focused invocation and anchoring of light within earth and humanity. Spreading information about the current unfolding plan, and how people can contribute to it, is highly valuable and essential work.

Creating Critical Mass

We are reaching a critical mass now that we can amplify through sharing what we are learning about the plan for transfiguration from outer sources, as well as from our own meditation impressions and intuition.

It is important to remember that the American Revolution was really fought by only 5 or 6% of the American population, and that success established a whole new level of freedom in the world. Social scientists say it only takes approximately 10% of a population to change a paradigm. Sociologist Paul Ray has found that between 30–35% of the U.S. population are orienting their lives around social justice, the environment, and spirituality, so we are already well on our way to the new world and can build on what is already present.

Conclusion: The Significance of Anchoring Light

There are a vast number of groups working at varying levels and degrees of subtle energy and significance, bringing in light and supporting the unfolding plan. Each is sourced from varying levels of purity of motive, with their corresponding degrees of spiritual effectiveness.

The greater the intention to serve and uplift the good of all life, without personal agendas, the more that light and love is able to radiate through these individuals and groups to the world. It is a useful part of every conscious light worker's service to seek out, identify and support those groups offering pure service.

The lighted sphere that is being created by the intensifying activity of all of these groups is a focal point for the Light Alliance. The frequency, expansiveness and intensity of the light present is the determining factor for launching the Day of Revelation. Thus, the invocation and distribution of light by each individual light worker and group has cosmic significance.

The growth of light and love within this earth sphere is being closely observed by all levels of the Light Alliance, from the spiritual Masters to the Galactics. At the level of the Solar Being there is great rejoicing, as earth, humanity, the Earth Light Alliance and the Galactic Light Alliance prepare to throw off the final veils of darkness to emerge as a lighted world. All has been prepared and is in readiness for humanity and the earth to emerge into the light, love and joy and freedom of the fifth dimension.

The spiritual Masters have worked for millennia for this synthesis of worlds, and are anticipating the freeing of earth with great joy as well. Humanity will be astonished and stand in amazement as the revelations unfold for all. You can continue to visualize and live in the reality of this glorious future, and watch it unfold towards you with joy, anticipation and thanksgiving.

This is being shared to inspire you about the ultimate impact of every thought, word and action you create in this current intensified phase of world transfiguration. Each of us, and each group with which we may be affiliated, have our chosen field of service and contribution. Our inner process of contact and interaction with our soul has guided us into our placement within this great movement of light. In the fulfillment of each individual's and each group's self-chosen sphere of radiation, the planet is being lighted, and the transfiguration is taking place.

Know that we have the assistance of mighty cosmic forces and powers, which guarantees our ultimate success. We can base our faith and unshakable confidence on this cosmic power with which we are aligned. Place your trust in it, go forward in your life and work with vision, joy and love, and rest assured that all is unfolding in fulfillment of the highest good and greater plan. In doing so, individually and collectively, we are making an essential contribution to the transfiguration of our world into the new earth.

A SPECIAL GIFT

For *The Transfiguration of Our World* Readers

A message from the author:

If you find the ideas, perspectives and meditations in this book valuable, I would like to offer you a special gift:

My guided **Soul Contact audio meditation** on how you can connect with higher guidance for your life.

All you need to do is go to our website at www.worldtransfiguration.com, enter your name and email address, then download an MP3 file, and listen to my inspiring and centering meditation to connect with your soul and call in higher guidance for your life. You can also download a written form of the meditation for your use.

I know you will find this meditation very helpful, as many people have told me they deeply appreciate the meditations I offer to help them connect with their higher self and bring through spiritual guidance and support.

Here is some feedback on the Soul Contact meditation:

> "I can't thank you enough! I am so grateful! You helped me in a way that I've rarely encountered. You gave me the meditation to bring my soul into my heart - every minute of the day - and live from there.
>
> I've been practicing it to the best of my ability. And it is clearly helping me to stay mindful of being "full" and returning quickly to it when I notice that I'm not. I feel a big difference in my mood and attitude. You are brilliant!"
>
> Michelle Bendowski, consulting client

Go to www.worldtransfiguration.com to download this meditation now.

About the Author

Gordon Asher Davidson is the President and co-founder of the Center for Visionary Leadership based in San Rafael, CA and Phoenix, AZ. He has been a founder and Director of three non-profit organizations, and is a nationally recognized author and lecturer who has been teaching and lecturing on social change and spiritual development for over 38 years.

He is co-author with his wife, Corinne McLaughlin, of *The Practical Visionary, Spiritual Politics* (foreword by the Dalai Lama), and *Builders of the Dawn.* He is a Fellow of the World Business Academy and the Findhorn Foundation in Scotland, and a member of the Transformational Leadership Council.

Gordon has served as the founding Director of The Social Investment Forum, a national association of investment professionals, money market funds and community loan funds, and of the Coalition for Environmentally Responsible Economies (CERES), a coalition of social investment professionals, environmentalists, religious and labor leaders.

As a co-founder and former president of Sirius, an educational and spiritual community on 93 acres in Massachusetts, Gordon helped establish a pioneering ecological village for sustainable development and spiritual and environmental education in 1978, which is still thriving today.

Gordon has been an educator for many years, having served on the adjunct faculty of the Department of Government at American University in Washington, D.C.; and on the adjunct faculty of the Department of Anthropology of the University of Massachusetts.

He has lectured at over 200 universities, churches, government agencies and educational centers in the United States and Europe over the last 38 years, including Harvard University, Cornell University, The U.S. Department of State, The World Future Society, and The California Institute of Integral Studies. He has been interviewed in over 130 newspapers, magazines and radio and television shows, including The New York Times, The Washington Post, The Wall Street Journal, USA Today, NBC TV and Fox News.

He has been a meditator and student of the Ageless Wisdom of East and West for over 45 years, teaching meditation and courses in spiritual development in the U.S. and Europe. He is a spiritual guide and consultant, assisting individuals and groups worldwide to access deep, inner levels of personal transformation, group leadership and higher guidance.

As a consultant and coach in personal growth, leadership, ethical decision making and team-building, Gordon has consulted with many private, public and non-profit leaders and organizations.

His rich and varied journey through many years as a spiritual explorer and pioneering social activist, creating organizations and spiritual communities, led him to the realization that many dimensions of human life are simply not consciously recognized or understood. The progression of his meditative life over 50 years has led him into contact with the inner dimensions described in detail in this book.

For More Information

Gordon offers teleseminars, presentations and private coaching on how you can benefit from and co-create with the world transfiguration currently underway. This includes how to facilitate the infusion of light into your being, clear old patterns in your subconscious, and raise your frequency.

He also offers updates on the future of our world and how we each can contribute to its creation. If you are interested in participating in his ongoing groups and seminars, or private coaching, or inviting him to speak to your group, please contact him through:

Email: worldtransfiguration@gmail.com
Website: www.worldtransfiguration.com

Made in the USA
San Bernardino, CA
15 August 2016